THE LITTLE GIANT

The Story of Johnny Griffin

THE LITTLE GIANT

The Story of Johnny Griffin

Mike Hennessey

Northway publications

Published in 2008

Northway Publications
39 Tytherton Road, London N19 4PZ, UK.
www.northwaybooks.com

© Mike Hennessey 2008 (except Foreword)
© Orrin Keepnews 2008 (Foreword)

The right of Mike Hennessey to be identified as author of this work has been asserted by him in accordance with the Copyright, Designs and Patents Act 1988.

The publishers acknowledge with thanks the kind permission of copyright holders to reprint the photographs used in this book. Permissions have been sought in all cases where the identity of copyright holders is known. Photos by David Redfern are ©David Redfern/Redferns.

A CIP record for this book is available from the British Library.

ISBN 978 0955090 5 1

Printed and bound in Great Britain by Cromwell Press Ltd, Trowbridge, Wiltshire.

Contents

Other books by Mike Hennessey

Some of My Best Friends Are Blues by Ronnie Scott with Mike Hennessey, illustrations by Wally Fawkes and Mel Calman, republished by Northway Publications, 2004

Klook: The Story of Kenny Clarke, Quartet Books, 1990

Tin Pan Alley by Eddie Rogers, as told to Mike Hennessey, Robert Hale Ltd, 1964

Foreword

I have been involved in producing jazz albums for what seems to be an unbelievably long time – I began in 1954, so at this time of writing it has been going for more than a half-century. Some of the most important personal friendships in my life have developed from the working relations involved in planning and recording that music. Certainly one of the oldest and strongest of these is the bond between Johnny Griffin and myself. It has survived not only the passage of time and countless working hours in a great many recording studios under a wide variety of circumstances, but also a vast amount of geography, as I relocated from New York to San Francisco and he far outdid me by moving from New York and Chicago to the south of France.

The first time I ever heard of Johnny Griffin probably should have indicated that I was likely to keep on hearing about him for quite some time although I certainly could be forgiven for not realizing at the time that I would continue knowing and working with him just about for ever. Because the man who first mentioned Griffin to me was, at the time, certainly the most distinguished jazz musician I knew. Even now, more than two decades after his death, Thelonious Monk remains the most important artist I have ever had the pleasure of working with.

But, at that time, he had not yet succeeded in fighting his way through to broad recognition. Also, having run up against some of the arbitrary regulations that governed New York night life at the time, he was not licensed to work with any regularity in that city and, on this occasion, he had accepted an engagement to travel to Chicago by himself and appear with some local musicians he did not know. But the situation developed much better than it might have. The bassist on the job was Wilbur Ware, who would soon move to New York and work frequently with Monk over the next few years. And the group also included a young local tenor saxophone player named Johnny Griffin.

Monk, at the time, had begun what was to be an almost six-year association with Riverside Records, a very young independent jazz record label of which I was co-founder, co-owner and sole record producer. Like several of my colleagues in the jazz business, I really did not know what I was doing. I did, however, know enough to appreciate what it meant when Monk, recounting his adventures in Chicago, paid Griffin the considerable compliment of quietly declaring: 'He can play.'

But, as I soon discovered, this knowledge did me very little immediate good. Alfred Lion, founder of Blue Note Records, (who had been the first to record Monk), had already become aware of Griff and had signed him up to an exclusive contract. So I had to start by judiciously using Johnny as a sideman on other people's dates. I clearly recall the very first such occasion: it was our first album featuring the great Ellington trumpet player, Clark Terry – whom I had also met through Monk. I began to use the tenor player as often as possible on other people's dates and, sooner than I expected, he became fully available.

Perhaps because he continued to live in Chicago, possibly because (like a great many of the players whose importance has eventually become a recognized part of jazz history) his own records didn't particularly sell when they were new, and at least in part because he had made it clear to Blue Note that he would rather be with us, they made no real effort to extend his contract, and, in late February of 1958, he came to New York for what was to be the first of a great number of occasions we would work together in a recording studio. And, because transporting a musician from the Midwest was no small burden for our little label, I planned to make double use of Johnny's few days in New York – both as part of a Monk sextet date and leading a quartet on his own Riverside début as a leader.

As it turned out, however, our scheduled first studio evening turned into a major confusion of missed signals and lack of communication, so that the two key cast members of the Monk project never did appear and I was forced to do a lot of improvising and last-minute phone-calling – and finished the week with no Monk LP, but two by Johnny.

I originally planned to have Johnny Griffin appear on a Monk album while he was in New York to make his own first Riverside recording. The Monk session, as agreed with Thelonious, was to be a sextet date also involving Sonny Rollins, Donald Byrd, Art Blakey and Wilbur Ware. We arbitrarily divided responsibility for notifying these four men of time and place – I called Byrd and Ware, Thelonious was to contact Sonny and Blakey. (Remember that, at that time, no-rehearsal dates, completely constructed after the personnel were assembled in the studio, were not all that unusual.)

Rollins and Blakey did not appear and could not be reached for some time. Eventually both men claimed, quite believably, that Monk had never contacted them about the session. So we sought replacements. But after rehearsing and doing one or two takes on a new Monk composition, he decided that, since this wasn't the band he had intended to record with, he didn't want to continue – and he left. I then decided not to stop, since I was going to have to pay the musicians anyway. I reached Kenny Drew at his home – he was scheduled to be the pianist on Johnny's quartet album - and we did record most of a Griffin sextet LP that night.

Quite importantly, Monk at this time was in the midst of accomplishing a major breakthrough. Having been legally cleared for regular work in New York clubs by mid-1957, he quickly began his long and legendary stand at the Five Spot with a group that included John Coltrane. And when Trane, rapidly developing into a star in his own right, left after six months, Thelonious soon took advantage of the opportunity to back up his frequently expressed enthusiasm for Griffin by bringing Johnny into that quartet.

It must be admitted that, at this point, Griffin took a bit of a beating – primarily from the critics (fellow musicians and even club-owners knew better) – simply because he was himself and sounded like himself and not like his predecessor. But Monk knew how to draw the greatest benefits from working with Johnny. Thelonious may have been second only to Duke Ellington in his ability to adapt his band's repertoire and arrangements to fit the strengths and special abilities of valuable sidemen – and quite concrete evidence of that exists on two very exciting Riverside albums that were recorded in performance at the Five Spot one night in August 1958.

I very much enjoyed working with Griff on a variety of projects. He was one of the first jazz musicians from whom I learned that what you hear in their music can be not just art, but real emotion. The warmth, the wit, the joy or sadness that certain players project is a direct expression of the man himself. (Griffin has always been such a direct communicator; Wes Montgomery was another, so that the night on which they were recorded together at a Berkeley, California club for Wes's Full House album on Riverside was a most memorable example of that particular form of soulfulness.) One of our goals was to overcome the stereotype of the slogan that some writers had pinned on Johnny as 'The fastest gun in the west'.

As one step in that direction, I approved the unrealistic expense of a 1959 with-strings and almost-all-ballads LP called White Gardenia, which was undoubtedly one of the first Billie Holiday memorials. The excitement generated by the distinctive two-tenor team of Johnny and Eddie 'Lockjaw' Davis impressed a lot of people, but it wasn't exactly an all-out commercial success. (I clearly remember Griffin's exasperation when a booking agent proudly announced the price he had been able to get the quintet for a week's work – it was exactly what Johnny had received for his own quartet the preceding year!)

Eventually, for that and other personal reasons, Griffin began paying attention to the success that comparable (or lesser) jazz musicians were enjoying in Europe – and, eventually, he was gone.

I did not see Johnny again for about a decade and a half, but when he made his first return visit to the United States, to appear at the 1978 Monterey Jazz Festival, I drove him back to San Francisco and, a day later, he was in a studio at Fantasy Records, where I was then running the jazz programme, as a featured guest on a Nat Adderley album that happened to duplicate the 1958 circumstances of Nat's first Riverside album – a quintet date with Griff as the other horn.

Over the years, that sort of thing has continued – every now and then we make a record together. Whenever we are in the same part of the world, we make a real effort to hang out together, to eat or drink or listen to music. My wife died in late 1989; one of my fondest mementos remains a picture of the two of us at a table in a Bay Area jazz club. Our friend Johnny is there with us, though not visible in the photo, and we are both laughing heartily at some now unremembered punch line he has just delivered.

Johnny Griffin is both a talented musician and a valuable human being. Mike Hennessey, who has known him for a long time, has done an admirable job of setting down for his readers both sets of qualities.

Orrin Keepnews

Preface

Not least among the achievements of Johnny Griffin, the Little Giant from the South Side of Chicago, is that he has remained at the top of his game despite having spent the last thirty-five years of his sixty-two-year playing career as a resident of Europe.

It has happened all too often in jazz that when an American star takes up residence in Europe, he gradually becomes absorbed into the European scene and his star status slowly but surely ebbs away. Not so with Griffin. He is still recognised internationally as a legendary jazz icon with a readily identifiable style, unblemished integrity, an immense improvisational flair and an unfailing capacity to swing. As British writer Brian Priestley has observed in his *Jazz: The Rough Guide*:

'Although Griffin is fully conversant with the tenor tradition of Hawkins, Byas, Webster and Young, it has often been remarked how close in spirit Griffin's playing is to that of Charlie Parker. The headlong rush of ideas and the rhythmic variety and freedom that go with them, all point in this direction. In addition, his tone combines a vocalised sound with a slightly hysterical edge that, at his best, can evoke almost uncontrollable exhilaration – except, perhaps, for other tenor players, since Griffin is one of the fastest and most accurate ever on his instrument.'

Reviewing a Johnny Griffin performance in *Down Beat* in 1958, Ralph J. Gleason wrote: 'Unquestionably, Johnny Griffin can play the tenor saxophone faster, literally, than anyone else alive. At least, he can claim this until it's demonstrated otherwise. And in the course of playing with this incredible speed, he also manages to blow longer without refuelling than you would ordinarily consider possible. With this equipment, he is able to play almost all there could possibly be played in any given chorus.'

Commenting on Gleason's statement in his note for the March 1967 Black Lion album, *The Man I Love*, Alun Morgan observed:

'As far as it goes, Gleason's words are probably correct. (In the absence of a jazz section to the *Guinness Book of Records*, we must assume Griffin's leading position in the field of runners in the Semi-Quaver Race.) But it would be wrong to assume that John Arnold Griffin III was nothing more than a note-producing machine. He is an amazingly consistent soloist, a man who is never off form by all accounts; undeniably he likes fast tempos but is a complete, rounded jazz musician, capable of tackling any material. Since he came to Europe in 1962, at the age of thirty-four, he has been giving free lessons on the gentle arts of relaxation, saxophone technique, deep-seated emotional intensity and a host of other important elements to thousands of listeners in Paris, London, Copenhagen and any other centers where jazz is appreciated.'

Johnny Griffin is not particularly disturbed by being called, 'the fastest gun in the west'. He says, 'I like to play fast. I get excited, and I have to sort of control myself, restrain myself. But when the rhythm section gets cooking, I want to explode.' He told Israeli journalist Ben Shalev in December 2005: 'I don't care at all if they describe me like that. It's definitely not insulting, and if it's good publicity, why not? After all, it's just a label. It's like there was a period when they called me 'the little giant'. There's no need to take those descriptions too seriously. As far as I'm concerned, they can call me 'the big midget'.'

Whatever fanciful appellation is used to describe him, there is absolutely no doubt that Johnny Griffin is one of the supreme masters of the tenor saxophone – an uncompromising swinger whose energy and creative vitality are unsurpassed.

One of the salient characteristics of Griffin's improvisational style is his predilection for decorating his solos with phrases borrowed from well-known, and predominantly unlikely, compositions. On a live recording made with Sal Nistico and Roman Schwaller in Munich in 1985 (*Three Generations of Tenor Saxophone*, JHM Records), the Little Giant managed to include in his solos extracts from 'The Yellow Rose of Texas', a Chopin 'Polonaise', Charlie Parker's 'Cool Blues', 'The Surrey with the Fringe on Top', Mendelssohn's 'Wedding March', 'The Foggy, Foggy Dew', 'The Kerry Dancers', Thelonious Monk's 'Rhythm-a-ning', 'Mairzy Doats', 'Turkey in the Straw' and 'Rhapsody in Blue' (see Appendix: 'Quotes').

Johnny is celebrated for his sterling work with Art Blakey and Thelonious Monk, for his 'blow-torch' duets with Eddie 'Lockjaw' Davis, for his inspired and electrifying work with the Clarke–Boland Big Band in the late 1960s and early 1970s, and for a diverse flock of admirable albums recorded for an assortment of labels with small groups, which he has always favoured. He says he prefers to work with a quartet because it gives him the maximum possible freedom: 'I can change heads when I feel like it – but with another horn in the group there has to be a little more control, and so less space for creativity. With just a rhythm section, I can do what I want. The musicians I idolised as a youth were Lester Young and Ben Webster – they worked with just rhythm sections – and that's the format that I like.'

When he's on the stand, holding forth at high speed with a sensitive and supportive rhythm section, Johnny Griffin is in his element. An uncompromising believer in straight-ahead, hard-swinging jazz, he says: 'As long as guys swing, jazz will not die.' Jazz music is Griffin's religion. And he has some very firm opinions about some of the musicians who operate on the free side of the jazz spectrum.

As he said to me in a 1979 interview for *Jazz Journal International*:

'You get all this talk about avant-garde music, but who plays it apart from guys in a few lofts in New York and one or two guys in Europe? I can't imagine them going into Harlem and playing that stuff. They'd get lynched.

'I have given this a great deal of thought ever since I heard Archie Shepp for the first time, every night for a month at Le Chat Qui Pêche in Paris. That band sounded as sad at the end of the month as it did at the beginning – but I understood even less.

'And how can people take Ornette Coleman's trumpet and violin playing seriously? Come on, that's just ridiculous.'

Griffin is one of the most articulate of musicians – both verbally and instrumentally. Whether he is having a conversation or holding forth on the tenor saxophone, he tells it like it is. Johnny Griffin speaks his mind. He is a genial cynic and a down-to-earth realist with a quick-fire wit and a great sense of humour. He says of himself: 'I'm a Taurus – like Duke Ellington and Joe Henderson – we eat too much, drink too much and love too much. Very stubborn.'

Johnny has long been a popular favourite at major festivals around the globe. He still commands a substantial and enthusiastic international following and is in constant demand for festival, concert and club dates. He has an immutable musical philosophy, which he outlines as follows: 'I'm happy with what I do because I feel good doing it – and that's the most important thing. I'm not following anybody – I'm just playing the music I want to play. If people dig it, that makes me doubly happy.'

Johnny Griffin's move to Europe forty-four years ago was a matter of survival. He often said, unequivocally, that had he not moved to Europe for good in 1963, he would not have survived for more than a year or so. As he put it, in a mid-1960s interview: 'If I had stayed in America I would be dead by now. I was a stoned zombie when I left.'

As well as expressing himself with great verve and vitality through his tenor saxophone, Johnny Griffin is a witty and entertaining conversationalist with an unending flow of anecdotal reminiscences about his days with Lionel Hampton, Art Blakey, Thelonious Monk, Eddie 'Lockjaw' Davis, the Clarke–Boland Big Band and the variety of small groups he has fronted over the years. He is a natural optimist and, at the same time, a thoroughgoing realist, with a healthy scepticism when it comes to promoters, politicians and jazz pundits.

He is a compassionate man, completely lacking in arrogance, and is also a perceptive observer of the world at large and an avid reader who takes a keen interest in international affairs. He is a man who lives life to the full and who has been a good friend to the distillers over the years.

He once told me, back in September 1965:

'You know, I was drinking a bottle of gin a day at one time. Now I've got it down to five double whiskies a night – but it is still too much. Alcohol gives you a lift, deadens the nerves, gets rid of inhibitions. Whisky can make a poor man feel like a millionaire. That's why they sell so much of the stuff!'

Apropos the lubricating oil, an encounter I had with Johnny at the Jazz Land club in Paris in September 1965 produced a characteristic Griffinism, which should not go unrecorded:

'How,' I asked, 'can you play so ridiculously well when you are stoned?'

'You see, baby,' Johnny replied, 'I was stoned when I learnt to play!'

And in a June 2005 interview, when I asked him what he considered to be the real high points of his career, he replied, 'I think it would be all the bars I was introduced to over the years. I lost count . . . or perhaps I should say, I lost consciousness.'

We got onto the subject of playing, and Johnny said that he tries to play what he feels rather than what he thinks. 'I'm always doing things I've never heard of or played before. Of course, there are always times when you are not creating, when the clichés come out. Sometimes I can see myself going into a familiar phrase, but it starts so fast I can't stop it – so I'll try to vary it a little. But I don't like getting too 'mental' about this because it makes the music too contrived. When it gets good is when something takes over my mind. Sometimes it feels as though my mind leaves my body and I seem to have nothing to do with the music that's coming out. It's as though somebody else has taken over.'

'Johnny Walker?' I asked. And he roared.

'Or Glen Grant. But if I'm really hot, I can play just about everything I feel. I just like to let the music flow out.'

The story of Johnny Griffin is a light-hearted, irreverent and uninhibited look back at the jazz life of one of the music's most consummate musicians and one of its most colourful and entertaining characters. And it is the story of a man who is totally committed to his craft.

Mike Hennessey,
Durchhausen, Germany,
January, 2008

Acknowledgements

I would like to record my grateful thanks to Miriam and Johnny Griffin for their wholehearted co-operation and to Orrin Keepnews, David Redfern, Gigi Campi, Nathan Davis, Jimmy Woode, Alan Bates and Fabienne Herenberg of SACEM for their valued contributions to this biography.

My thanks, too, to the following for the use of material in taped interviews with Johnny Griffin: Ben Sidran, National Public Radio, USA, 1998; Mark Vasey, CKUA Radio Educational, Edmonton, Alberta, Canada, December 5th 1979; Digby Fairweather, BBC Radio 2, August 1991; FM88 Jazz Radio, Long Beach, California, USA, April 27th 1989; Yvonne Seguin, *Inside Jazz*, CKLN Toronto, Canada, May 5th 1991; James Browne, WBGO Newark, New Jersey, USA, November 14th 1983; Joe Farmer, *Du Côté de Chez Swing*, Radio France, April 28th 1992; Peter Pullman, Verve Records, New York, USA, May 10th 1994; WBFO, Buffalo, New York, USA; Bill Goldberg, WKCR-FM, USA, June 27 1979; Billy Banks, WKCR-FM, USA, October 2nd 1980; Bob Bernotas, New York freelance writer and jazz historian, 1994 interview with Johnny Griffin, revised 1999.

I am also grateful for the use of the following written sources: African American Music Collection, Interviews with Johnny Griffin, October 9th and 30th 1982 by James A Standifer, University of Michigan School of Music; Dempsey J. Travis, *An Autobiography of Black Jazz*, Urban Research Institute Inc., Chicago, 1983; Arthur Taylor, *Notes And Tones*,

1978; Bill Moody, *The Jazz Exiles*, University of Nevada Press, 1993; Alwyn & Laurie Lewis, *Cadence*, December 1993; Max Jones, *Talking Jazz*, The Macmillan Press, 1987.

And, above all, my grateful thanks to my wife Gaby for her love and inspiration, her patience and her unfailing moral support.

M. H.

1

Sweet Home Chicago

My kind of town, Chicago is
My kind of town, Chicago is
My kind of razzmatazz
And it has, all that jazz.[1]

Chicago in the 1920s was a thriving jazz metropolis with a turbulent background of organized crime and a vast traffic in bootleg liquor. The city was dominated by gangland syndicates, which ran many of the cabarets, dancehalls and night clubs, where jazz was much in demand. These venues provided a lively and stimulating environment for some of the great jazz exponents of the period. Audiences were principally black during the week, but seventy-five per cent white on weekends.

King Oliver, who came to Chicago from New Orleans in 1918, played in the Royal Gardens Café (which later became the Lincoln Gardens Café), the Pekin and the Plantation; Jimmie Noone and Earl Hines worked at the Nest and the Apex, and Jelly Roll Morton appeared in the Richelieu, the DeLuxe and the Elite Café. Louis Armstrong, whom King

Oliver brought to Chicago in the summer of 1922, played at the Sunset and the Savoy Ballroom. In 1924 Louis joined Fletcher Henderson in New York but, the next year, he returned to Chicago and made the historic Hot Five and Hot Seven recordings there over the following three years – a period which many consider to have been the most creative of Armstrong's career.

Chicago's jazz explosion was boosted by the migration north of thousands of African Americans. As documented in the Chicago Jazz Archive of the University of Chicago Library, 'The Great Migration', as it came to be known, was triggered by a number of different factors – failing crops, racial discrimination, the prospect of relatively well-paid jobs in Chicago factories, and advertisements in the *Chicago Defender*, which promised a better life 'up north'.

Between 1916 and the end of the 1920s, at least seventy-five thousand southern immigrants arrived on the South Side of Chicago, and a substantial number of New Orleans jazz and blues musicians joined in this exodus, following the closure in 1917 of that city's notorious Storyville district by the US Navy. This resulted in the ultimate disappearance of most of New Orleans' bars, honky-tonks and speakeasies where jazz had once flourished.

The vast majority of the African American immigrants settled in a narrow corridor on the South Side, between 16th and 39th Streets – an area of dilapidated housing, bounded by State Street to the east and the Rock Island Railroad tracks and LaSalle Street to the west, which became known as the Black Belt.

The first moves towards nationwide liquor prohibition in the United States began in December 1917, when Congress adopted the Eighteenth Amendment which banned the manufacture, sale and transportation of alcoholic drinks. The Amendment was ratified in January 1919 and, after being approved by thirty-six states, went into effect in January 1920. This provided the perfect opportunity for Chicago's gangs – and for Al 'Scarface' Capone's mafia mob in particular – to exploit the ban and satisfy the ever-growing demand for booze through the city's many clubs and speakeasies. At one time, Capone, who was said to have been a lover of jazz and classical music, was making $60 million a year from the sale of alcoholic drinks alone.

In his book, *An Autobiography of Black Jazz*, published by the Chicago-based Urban Research Institute in 1983, Dempsey J. Travis notes that Chicago, New York and Kansas City housed a disproportionate percentage of all the great jazz talent in America during the 1920s and 1930s. 'These cities,' he writes, 'were controlled by the Jazz Slave Masters and some of the very best black musicians were their serfs. Talented jazz musicians were chained to bands and specific night clubs and saloons in the same manner as the antebellum Negroes were shackled to plantations.'

Travis observes that at the Grand Terrace Ballroom and other Chicago night-spots, terminating an engagement without the authorization of the management was a health hazard to many Chicago jazzmen. This was why Earl Hines remained at the Grand Terrace Ballroom for more than a decade.

The Grand Terrace, on South Parkway, was one of a number of nightspots for which African American musicians were in demand but to which access by black jazz fans was denied. In his interview in the Dempsey Travis book, Cab Calloway argues, rather unexpectedly, that this racist policy had a positive aspect. He says, 'I doubt seriously if jazz could have survived if black musicians hadn't gone along with the racial practices of Harlem's Cotton Club and Connie's Inn, Chicago's Grand Terrace and many other clubs throughout America that entertained white patrons with black jazz artists.'

'Remember,' Travis explains, 'that the Jazz Slave Masters always controlled the cash register, paid the piper and called the tune. The keepers of the cash box were usually Jewish or Italian and, occasionally, they were mob-connected blacks. The creators of jazz music were black. All of this had a positive side. Whenever there was a generous segment of Jews, Italians or blacks co-existing within an urban area, the results favoured jazz music.'

However, many of Chicago's leading jazz exponents were white. In his book, *The Making Of Jazz*,[2] James Lincoln Collier recalls that, in the 1920s, an important group of white musicians, inspired by the Original Dixieland Jazz Band, was coalescing in the Midwest. It became known as the Chicago school of jazz because some of its principal members had attended Chicago's Austin High School (the Austin High School gang) and because the city was offering plenty of working opportunities for jazz groups.

The musicians came from various parts of the Midwest – Bix Beiderbecke from Davenport, Iowa; Frankie Trumbauer from Carbondale, Illinois; Eddie Condon from Goodland, Indiana; Frank Teschemacher from Kansas City; George Wettling from Topeka, Kansas; Red McKenzie and Pee Wee Russell from St. Louis, Missouri. Some came from even further afield – like Wingy Manone from New Orleans, and Max Kaminsky from Brockton, Massachusetts. Others, such as Benny Goodman, Jimmy McPartland, Dave Tough, Joe

Sullivan, Bud Freeman, Gene Krupa and Muggsy Spanier, were native to Chicago and its environs.

At first, the Chicagoans simply copied the style of King Oliver and the New Orleans Rhythm Kings, but, in some cases, they brought to it a superior instrumental technique (Goodman) and a more vigorous and extrovert rhythmic style (Krupa), together with a greater emphasis on solo playing. In general, however, they added variations to the basic features of New Orleans jazz rather than endeavouring to develop an independent style.

Two of the first white bands to come north were those of trombonist Tom Brown, which opened at Lamb's Café on May 15th 1915, and Stein's Dixie Jass Band, led by drummer Johnny Stein, which opened at Schiller's Café on March 3rd 1916. The Dixie Jass Band was the quintet which later became the Original Dixieland Jazz – or Jass – Band, with Tony Sbarbaro replacing Stein on drums and cornettist Nick LaRocca taking over as leader.

These two groups made a big impact in Chicago. Working in cafés and cabarets that regularly presented white entertainers, they attracted a good deal of attention. In January 1917, the ODJB went to New York and made the very first jazz recordings – 'Livery Stable Blues' and 'Dixie Jass Band One-Step' – for the Victor Talking Machine Company, on February 26th.

Jazz played by white-only bands was one of the most popular presentations of the Chicago Theater, a movie house run by the Balaban brothers and Morris Katz. Faced by severely declining attendance figures, they launched their first Syncopation Week in September 1922 – and it was a huge success. The jazz concerts drew big crowds to the theatre, irrespective of the quality of the movie being shown, and it quickly became one of the most popular places for the more conservative white Chicagoans – those who tended to avoid dance halls, night clubs and speakeasies – in which to enjoy live jazz. Weekly gross revenues at the Chicago Theater were, on average, fifty per cent higher when jazz was included as part of the show.

When John Arnold Griffin III came into the world on April 24th 1928, Chicago had established itself as the jazz capital of the United States. Given the potency of his inherent musical aptitude and background, plus the environment of an intensely jazz-orientated city, it was no surprise that, before he was out of his teens, Johnny Griffin elected to pursue a career as a professional jazz musician.

He was born at Providence Hospital on 51st Street, a medical establishment founded by black Chicagoans, and was brought up in the home of his grandmother, at 432 East 46th Street, a brownstone house in a middle-class African American district on Chicago's South Side. This same street also housed the offices of Oscar DePriest, a member of the Republican Party, who was the first African American to serve on the city council of Chicago and, on November 6th 1928, became the first African American to win a seat in the United States House of Representatives. It was Congressman DePriest who, some fifteen years later, would help Johnny Griffin buy his first saxophone.

Other near-neighbours included Dinah Washington (then known by her true name, Ruth Lee Jones) and Mahalia Jackson (both of whom sang at a local Baptist church), Ray Nance and Milt Hinton. Johnny Griffin was to meet up again with Dinah Washington some years later when he joined the Lionel Hampton band.

Johnny Griffin's father, John Arnold Griffin II, who came from Alabama and worked in a steel mill, was an amateur cornet player and a regular member of the marching band run by the black newspaper, the *Chicago Defender*. The band used to play in the black neighbourhood on the South side, taking part in parades by members of the Masonic-style organization, the Elks, and also in the Easter Parades. He gave up playing after his son was born, so Johnny never got to hear his father play. 'But I did find one of his mouthpieces,' says Johnny, 'and I used to buzz it.'

Johnny's mother, known to everyone as 'Billy', was born Willie Zelda Greenup and came from Chetwin, Louisiana. She played piano, mainly for church functions, and was also a regular member of the choir of St. John Baptist, a church on 48th Street and Michigan Avenue. But his parents' relationship was a troubled one and they separated before he had reached his fourth birthday – so Johnny never really got to know his father.

He recalls, 'As a child I was always surrounded by music. There were records in the house by Jimmie Lunceford, Don Byas, Coleman Hawkins, Chick Webb, Ben Webster, Lester Young, Ellington, Basie, Artie Shaw and Benny Goodman, which we played on an old wind-up Victrola. I started listening to jazz records when I was four years old and the band that impressed me most at that time was Duke Ellington's.

'When I was six, I began taking piano lessons from my Great Uncle Pace, who was a devotee of religious music. Later on, he moved to Pittsburgh and I then took lessons from Sterling Todd, who was organist at the Savoy Ballroom. He was also the pianist with Doc Cook and his fourteen Doctors of Syncopation, a band which played in the Casino at Chicago's White City amusement park.'

Johnny took piano lessons for about four years and soon followed in his mother's footsteps, playing piano for church teas and in the Sunday school – songs like 'Old Black Joe' and 'Swanee River'. One of his mother's favourite songs was the Peter De Rose/Mitchell Parish composition, 'Deep Purple', and this was the first tune he learned to play on the piano.

When he was eight years old, a neighbour began teaching him Hawaiian steel guitar – not an instrument for which he had much affection. 'His name was Mr Burns. He was an excellent teacher and he taught me church music and some Bing Crosby songs like 'Sweet Leilani'. But I really wanted to play a wind instrument,' says Johnny.

At the age of nine, he attended a weekly, one-hour music appreciation class and listened to classical music – by Bach, Brahms, Tchaikovsky, Beethoven – all the great classical composers. He says, 'That was a good grounding. These days, I don't listen too much to jazz records. I like to listen to music by Prokofiev, Stravinsky, Tchaikovsky, Bartók, Shostakovich and Sibelius – and I especially love Ravel and Debussy.'

Griffin was thirteen when he fulfilled his wish to play a wind instrument. He rented a clarinet for four dollars a month and he began taking lessons. Three years earlier, he had had the opportunity to hold a saxophone in his hands, and it was at that moment that he knew that there could be no other wind instrument for him. His Aunt Rose, a dancer with Nat King Cole's *Shuffle Along* touring revue, was married to a saxophone player, and when Johnny went to visit the couple, his uncle showed him the saxophone and, tantalizingly, let him hold it, but didn't allow him to try playing it – though Johnny was completely fascinated by the instrument.

At this time, he was attending the Forestville Elementary School, mid-way between the homes of his mother and his father, and he would spend weekdays with his mother and weekends with his father. When he graduated in June 1941, his class had a party at the Parkway Ballroom, where the music was provided by the band of King Kolax (William Little), a twenty-three-year-old trumpet player who had studied at the Wendell Phillips High School and who, four years later, became a member of the legendary Billy Eckstine Orchestra. The tenor saxophone soloist with Kolax was sixteen-year-old Gene Ammons, an alumnus of DuSable High School and the son of the renowned pioneer boogie-woogie pianist, Albert Ammons. 'When I heard Gene play,' says Johnny, 'I absolutely knew that I was going to be a tenor saxophone player – not a shred of doubt.'

According to Johnny, three of the main jazz clubs during his time in Chicago were the Rhumboogie, the Club De Lisa and the Beige Room. The Rhumboogie was on the first floor of the Ritz Building on East Garfield Boulevard and was partly owned by the heavyweight boxer, Joe Louis. Roy Eldridge had an apartment on the third floor of the building. T-Bone Walker was a regular attraction at the club in the 1940s and Sarah Vaughan played there in 1946, packing the place every night. The Club De Lisa on State Street was owned by Italian immigrants, Mike, Louie and Jim De Lisa, who were heavily into the production of moonshine. The club opened in 1933 during the World's Fair. Albert Ammons and his

King Kolax

GRAND OPENING
GIGANTIC
BENEFIT
DANCE
Thursday
March 19th
9 P.M.
WHITE CITY
BALLROOM
63rd and South Parkway
MUSIC BY
KING KOLAX
AND HIS BAND
The Cooperative Club Sponsors
DANCE TICKETS ... 50c
AT DOOR ... 60c inc. tax
Tickets on sale at: Joe's Deluxe

Chicago Defender, March 14th 1942.

Rhythm Kings, with Israel Crosby on bass, played there in 1935 and among the later attractions were Joe Williams and Billy Eckstine. The Beige Room was in the basement of the Pershing Hotel at 64th and Cottage Grove Avenue. Among the major entertainers who appeared there were Earl Hines, Sonny Blount (Sun Ra) and Fritz Jones (Ahmad Jamal) who recorded his landmark double album, *Ahmad Jamal at the Pershing*, there in January 1958.

Johnny recalls, 'When I came up, there were a lot of places to play, many clubs and bars, and you could jam and sit in – on the South Side of Chicago alone there must have been at least twenty clubs, some of them very small and presenting just trios and quartets. There were other clubs in the centre and in the Loop and others on the North Side.'

He also remembers that, in the 1930s, racial discrimination was widespread. 'There would be white jazz in some clubs and black jazz in others. Entry to some places was restricted to white people and black people were not allowed in. There were Jim Crow practices in some of the theatres in the Loop. There weren't any signs indicating that black people had to sit in certain places, because that would have been a violation of the 1887 Civil Rights Act – but there were sections which were unofficially reserved for 'coloureds' and black people would be directed to these areas by the ushers.'

The Avenue Theater on South Indiana Street, which opened in August 1913, would allow only white people to occupy the stalls seats. The box office would tell black people that they could have access only to the balcony.

In a May 1977 interview with British writer Stan Woolley for *Cadence* magazine, Griffin said he first became aware of racial discrimination when he was about twelve or thirteen. 'And then I thought, "My God, this is crazy!" But, as a kid growing up, I never realized what was happening. We lived in a black neighbour-

Chicago Defender, September 12th 1942.

hood in Chicago. There the people were self-sufficient and so it was difficult to appreciate what was happening in the outside world until I went to high school – then I could see it. We would play football against a team of white kids and it was like warfare. It was terrible. Then, I used to work after school hours and had to go into the Italian, Polish or Jewish neighbourhoods, and, again, it was like war; I had to run out of those places. But, musically, it was beautiful. In America,

The Regal Theater,
4719 South Parkway Boulevard,
(later renamed Martin Luther
King Drive), Chicago, c. 1930.

the music departments in the schools are fantastic, whether you're white or black; that part of it was beautiful.'

His home was about two hundred yards away from the Regal Theater on South Parkway, a renowned, three thousand-seat entertainment venue which opened in February 1928 and which, over the years, presented some of the foremost names in jazz – among them, Louis Armstrong, Count Basie, Duke Ellington, Ella Fitzgerald, Billie Holiday, Nat King Cole, Jimmie Lunceford and Lena Horne. This was the theatre in which Johnny Griffin would make his début with the Lionel Hampton band at the age of seventeen.

'I remember that in 1955,' says Johnny, 'on 63rd Street there would be Miles in one club, the Messengers in another, Max Roach in another club, Ahmad Jamal in another, and me working in another, all in an area of about one acre – all these clubs. It was like 52nd Street [in New York] in the 1940s.'[3]

2

DuSable and Dyett

In September 1941, Johnny Griffin became a pupil at the DuSable High School on South Wabash Avenue in Chicago's black neighbourhood. The school, which had a total student population of around four thousand, was named after Jean Baptiste Point DuSable, a pioneer settler from the republic of Haiti, or Saint-Domingue as it was then known. Back in 1779, DuSable had built the first of Chicago's permanent settlements at the mouth of the Chicago River.

The school's music department was under the direction of Captain Walter Henri Dyett, an African American and an iconic figure, who was one of the very first music teachers in the United States to include jazz in a school's music curriculum. However, the term 'jazz' was never used in the early days because it was not considered appropriate for an academic institution.

In a teaching career spanning thirty years, Dyett was responsible for the musical education of more than twenty thousand students. As well as Johnny Griffin, the eminent jazz musicians who received their early training from him included trumpeter Sonny Cohn, trombonist Julian Priester,

Captain Walter
Dyett

saxophonists Gene Ammons, Von Freeman, John Gilmore, Eddie Harris, Joseph Jarman, Clifford Jordan and Laurdine 'Pat' Patrick, violinist Leroy Jenkins, pianists Nat King Cole and Dorothy Donegan, bassists Richard Davis, Milt Hinton, Fred Hopkins and Wilbur Ware, drummers Wilbur Campbell, Jerome Cooper and Walter Perkins, and singers Bo Diddley, Dinah Washington and Johnny Hartman.

Dyett, the son of a minister in the African Methodist Episcopal Church, was born in St. Joseph, Missouri, on January 11th 1901. After his family settled in California, he began studying violin and eventually became the concertmaster of his high school orchestra in Pasadena. He then engaged in two years of pre-medical studies but had to abandon these when his money ran out. He moved to Chicago in 1921 where he played with Erskine Tate's orchestra and conducted the orchestra at the Pickford Theater on Michigan Avenue.

In 1931, Dyett was appointed band director at the Wendell Phillips High School on East Pershing Road and, four years later, he became music director at the newly opened Jean Baptiste Point DuSable High School on South Wabash Avenue, with a syllabus covering classical, military and jazz music. He obtained a Bachelor of Music degree at Chicago's Vandercook College of Music in 1938 and a Master of Music degree at the Chicago Musical College in 1942. It was in the mid-1950s that he acquired the title 'Captain', for his service as director of the band of the Illinois National Guard.

He was an extraordinarily well-equipped teacher, with a phenomenal ear, the command of a great assortment of different instruments and a total commitment to his profession. A strict disciplinarian, who came down hard on students guilty of lapses of concentration, he was nevertheless a compassionate man who always had the best interests of his pupils at heart. He was spiritual mentor to a host of future professional musicians.

He also had his own professional ensemble which played for dances after school hours and, according to Griffin, it was a very good band. 'Dyett taught us discipline, to have respect for the music and to think of music as a profession, not a sport or a hobby. He insisted on our taking what we were doing very seriously. He could take kids off the street and mould them into young people with dignity and self-respect. He was like a father to his students, provided they took their work seriously, worked hard, paid attention and turned up on time. He didn't permit any displays of ego. Any student who was out of order would be told by Dyett, "Right, you are out of this class until you bring your mother and father to see me." That way, he involved the parents in their sons' education.'

Because the Chicago Board of Education would not provide musical instruments for his students, Dyett inaugurated an annual showcase for the student talent at DuSable – a musical revue with singers, dancers and comedians, which was called *High Jinks*. The show, which ran for four nights, drew audiences from all over the city. It was a high-level production, on a par with the professional shows staged at the Regal Theater, and it was so successful that it generated enough income to buy all the instruments Dyett needed. He gave each member of the show's band one dollar per night but, true to form, was unforgiving whenever there was a breach of his strict disciplinary code. Bassist Fred Hopkins once arrived five minutes late for a performance of *High Jinks* and was immediately fired from the band.

In an interview published in *An Autobiography of Black Jazz*, Dorothy Donegan recalled: 'Captain Dyett was an excellent musician and a hard taskmaster. He would always say, "When you're right, you can afford to keep quiet." But he also made you very conscious of being a good musician. He could hear a mosquito urinate on a bale of cotton. His musical ear was that sensitive . . . Out of a 150-piece concert band, he could tell exactly which instrument had made a mistake – and you would know it because he would stare at you and make you feel smaller than a snail.'

Eddie Harris said that Walter Dyett had to be tough and uncompromising because he had to deal with some pretty tough students: 'He just wouldn't tolerate you hitting a wrong note. I remember one time I fell asleep during a class. He kicked the chair out from under me and my clarinet went flying. But he was a great teacher. His programme began with the beginners' band, then there was the concert band, a marching band, a booster band and a booster orchestra. The booster band was a jazz ensemble and the booster orchestra was a pit band.'

Captain Walter Dyett
conducting a band of
DuSable students.

Harris added that he and fellow DuSable students, saxophonist John Gilmore, baritone saxophonist Laurdine 'Pat'
Patrick and trombonist Julian Priester, were all recruited by
Sun Ra for his band in the mid-1950s because they were such
excellent readers. Over the years, Woody Herman, Count
Basie, Duke Ellington and Lionel Hampton all visited the
school and were hugely impressed by the booster dance
band, which was a twenty-five-piece ensemble. 'It was so
accomplished,' said Harris, 'that if a name band hit town for
a date in one of the clubs or concert halls and was short of a
player because of the draft, or because of sickness, then they
would hire a student replacement – provided he was in the
union – and they could be sure that they wouldn't be let
down. Dyett really taught his students well.'

Dyett always insisted that the most important thing for
his students to master was sight-reading. Griffin remembers
that one feature of Dyett's instruction was that students had
to sing the band parts before playing them, even if they were
in one of the more advanced ensembles. And if they didn't

get good grades with their other subjects, they were not allowed to stay in the band.

Johnny Griffin had one goal above all others when he arrived at DuSable – to continue his musical education as a pupil of Walter Henry Dyett: 'I wanted to be taught by the man who taught Gene Ammons.' He made contact with Dyett at the first opportunity and asked to be enrolled in the band class. When he was asked by Dyett which instrument he wished to learn, Johnny answered, 'Tenor saxophone.' But, to his dismay, Dyett just laughed at the idea and told him, 'No, son, you can't play the tenor saxophone. In the first place, tenor saxophone is too large for you.'

Recalling that first meeting with Dyett, in a BBC Radio 2 interview with Digby Fairweather in August 1991, Griffin said, 'I was about four foot nine and weighed about sixty-five pounds. The Captain told me that if I wanted to be in the beginners' band, I had learn to play clarinet first.' Dyett regarded the clarinet as the father of all the reed instruments.

So, for his first six months at DuSable, Johnny Griffin played clarinet in the school's beginners' band, which he joined in September 1941. The band could have as many as 150 students, but if you made a good impression in this out-size ensemble, you graduated to the second concert band.

Johnny recalls having to take his mother to the school on one occasion: 'Dyett told her that I was learning the music too easily. Other kids were scuffling, but I was learning fast. He would hear me practising and he would come to me, and say, "Johnny, you're practising long, fast and strong. Slow down!"'

But Johnny Griffin had no wish to slow down, and he made such excellent progress at DuSable that, in January

1942, he was considered good enough to become a member of the second concert band. He then went through a daunting gamut of wind instruments. He started out playing third clarinet, but then Dyett switched him from B flat clarinet to alto clarinet, which is pitched in E flat, and then to bass clarinet. He also told Johnny that he must join the 100-piece Reserve Officers Training Corps band and add piccolo to his musical armoury. And finally, when the female oboe player graduated, Griffin was required to learn oboe. Later on, the band's English horn player graduated and, as Dyett didn't have a replacement, he made his star pupil take up this instrument too.

Several years later, Griffin would have cause to reflect that having learned to play such a plethora of wind instruments probably saved his life and that 'Dyett instilled a lot of music and a hell of a lot of discipline into me, because he still wouldn't let me get my hands on a saxophone.'

Having decided that Dyett was never going to allow him to play the instrument he dearly wished to concentrate on, Griffin bought himself a Wurlitzer alto saxophone by saving up the money he earned from delivering pamphlets and messages for Congressman Oscar DePriest. He remembers, 'You know, when I came up, the jazz in Chicago was very Kansas City rather than New Orleans-orientated. We were influenced by Count Basie and Jay McShann. And Chicago was predominantly a saxophone city. Most of the young musicians wanted to be saxophonists, largely inspired by Lester Young.'

In 1942 Griffin joined the Chicago branch of the American Federation of Musicians, Local 208. Because so many of the older musicians were being drafted into the armed forces, the union lowered the minimum age to fifteen.

Johnny was actually only fourteen, 'But,' he says, 'I suddenly aged a year.'

Local 208, which was chartered in 1902, was the first black musicians' labour organization to be created in the United States. Its affiliation with the American Federation of Musicians marked the beginning of the AFM's recognition of separate 'coloured' local offices. In Chicago, segregation effectively prevented black musicians from participating in the full range of musical performances. The situation was especially difficult for black classical musicians and did not improve until Local 208 merged with Local 10, the white union branch, some twenty years later.

Johnny began playing gigs in the local park and on street corners with guitarist George Freeman (brother of saxophonist Von Freeman), trumpeter James Higgins, bassist Leroy Jackson, drummer Wilbur Campbell and other young musicians. These pick-up bands would hustle tips from passers-by in return for playing requests.

'I remember the first professional gig I had,' Johnny told Dempsey J. Travis. 'It was a picnic for the Elks, the local branch of a Masonic-type fraternal organization, which advocated charity, justice, brotherly love, fidelity and American patriotism. They paid us 75 cents per man and I really thought I was a big shot then.'

Griffin went on to play gigs for McKee Fitzhugh, one of Chicago's principal dance promoters, who used to organize dances at the Parkway, the Pershing, the Trianon and White City ballrooms. Fitzhugh put together a group of fourteen or fifteen pieces called the Baby Band, which played dates around the South Side of Chicago. George Freeman, who was also in the band, recalled those early days in an interview with Nancy Wilson on National Public Radio in 1998:

Johnny Griffin with Milton Sneed (piano) and Leroy Jackson (bass) at Chicago's Pershing Ballroom, 1945.

'Johnny is not that tall and when he played alto saxophone it looked like he was playing baritone, because the alto was almost as large as he was. When it was time for Johnny to solo, he couldn't reach the mike because it was too high for him – so McKee Fitzhugh would stand him on a chair so that the bell of his horn could go into the mike. The people just went wild over that.'

It was during his spell with the Baby Band that Griffin first heard Charlie Parker. He remembers, 'My cousins were having a party in my house and they were playing this 1941 recording by Jay McShann – 'Hootie Blues' – with Walter

Brown taking the vocal. I heard Charlie Parker and, at first, I thought it was Lester. But then I thought, "No, it can't be, that's an alto." That was a magic moment for me.'

Johnny became the Baby Band's star soloist. In acknowledgement of this distinction, Fitzhugh put up a large poster of Griffin on the outside wall of Nick and Angels, a school store on the 49th Street side of DuSable High School, right across from the school band room on the third floor.

Says Johnny, 'I will never forget that. I was about four feet six inches tall and weighed only 105 pounds, but this picture on the wall made me look like a giant. You could see it when you looked out of the school's band room window – and, one day, Dyett really got on my case about it. This was when he had me playing oboe, because he had a programme of music by Ravel. I'd been given a part to learn, but hadn't practised it. There were about 130 students in the band room and, as I began tuning them up with the oboe, Dyett said to them, "Now, pay attention. I want to show you something. We have a star in the band. I want everyone to go over to the window and take a look to see who that star is." Then he said to me, "OK, star, play letter B." At this point my nerves were completely shot and I was fumbling around on the oboe like a total beginner. And Dyett said to the students, "Now you hear how the star plays!"

'Talk about putting me in my place – I was mortified. But, believe me, I could play the oboe damn well. I could play it in my sleep! Dyett would often taunt me about that poster. He'd say, "Hey, star, comb your hair," or, "Star, play this." Or, "Star, play that." He was giving me a hard time – but it was his way of keeping me from getting a big head.

'When he discovered that I was playing saxophone in McKee Fitzhugh's Baby Band, he allowed me to join the

DuSable booster band. The booster dance band played the school dances for graduations, proms and special school assemblies. I felt that I was moving up. But he still wouldn't let me play tenor saxophone, because he insisted it was too big for me. If you look at my old school photo, you'll see that when I sat in my chair in the booster band, my feet didn't touch the floor. Even worse, I sat next to Bill Atkins, who was so big that he made me look like a midget. I was playing alto in tenor style, because saxophonists at that time were all trying to imitate Ben Webster. On slow-tempoed numbers, I would try to play like Johnny Hodges, not realizing at the time that both Webster and Hodges really played the same way – except that one played tenor and the other played alto. But their styles were more or less the same. I was also very much influenced by Lester Young.'

In 1943, when he was fifteen, Griffin began playing with the Dallas-born pioneer blues guitarist and singer, T-Bone Walker, who had first come to Chicago a year earlier to head-line a revue at the Rhumboogie Club. The revue was such a success that T-Bone returned to the club year after year and recorded sides for the Rhumboogie label, with a band con-ducted by pianist/composer/arranger Marl Young. Griffin also played gigs with Walker at the El Grotto and the Club DeLisa and depped occasionally for alto and tenor saxophon-ist Johnny Board with the Dallas Bartley Orchestra at Joe's DeLuxe Café on 63rd Street and South Park. At this time he was attending school during the day and gigging almost every night.

Early in 1945, Johnny Griffin met Lionel Hampton, the bandleader with whom he began his full-time professional career. He remembers that in January or February of that year, 'the Hampton band was in Chicago for an engagement

Johnny Arnold Griffin as a young man: signed using the name he was called by some of his relatives, and given to his aunt.

at the Downtown Theater in the Loop. I was playing with the school band at what was called a pep assembly for some athletic event and Hamp came by the theatre together with his alto saxophonist, Herbie Fields, and pianist Milt Buckner.

'Captain Dyett chose some members from the booster band to join Hamp, Herbie and Buckner for a jam session. I was on alto, James Higgins was on trumpet, George Freeman on guitar and Lindal Marshall on drums. Hamp was clearly impressed by the way we played. At this particular time, he needed a saxophone player and he hired alto saxophonist Jay Peters, another Dyett protégé, who had come to DuSable from Englewood High School, where he had played in the senior band.'

However, Griffin's chance came in the summer of 1945, when the Lionel Hampton band returned to Chicago to play a one-week engagement at the Regal Theater. Jay Peters had been drafted into the US Navy, so Hampton was once more in need of a replacement saxophonist. Remembering Johnny Griffin's impressive jam session performance, he came to DuSable, sought Johnny out and asked him to join the band.

Griffin's natural aptitude, his unfaltering resolve to pursue a career in jazz and the rigorous educational regime of Walter Dyett combined to make him a perfect candidate to fill the vacancy in Hampton's saxophone section. Johnny recalls: 'I graduated from DuSable on a Thursday – June 26th 1945 – and, two days later, on June 28th 1945, I was playing with the Hampton band at the Regal Theater. The crazy thing was that I was making more money working on a Saturday night at the Pershing Hotel Lounge with my own sextet than I did with Hamp's band for a whole week!'

Walter Dyett continued as musical director at DuSable for a further sixteen years, retiring in 1961. It is generally agreed that none of his successors was able to equal him in the tremendously high standards of discipline and instruction that he pioneered. He died in 1969 and, in 1972, the Walter H. Dyett Academic Center was established in his honour on East 51st Street, in the middle of Washington Park.

3

Jivin' the Vibes

'King of the Vibes' Lionel Hampton was born in Louisville, Kentucky, on April 20th 1908. He was the son of pianist/vocalist Charles Hampton, who was killed in the First World War.

Lionel was given his first drum lessons by a Dominican sister in the Holy Rosary Academy, near Kenosha, Wisconsin, and continued his musical training at St. Monica's School in Chicago, where he got a job selling newspapers in order to join the Chicago Defenders' Newsboys Band, just as Johnny Griffin's father had done.

When he was twenty, Hampton moved to California and worked with the bands of Paul Howard, Eddie Barefield, Leon Elkins and Les Hite. It was in 1929 that he took up vibraphone, pioneering the instrument in the Elkins and Hite bands. The following year, the Hite band was hired to back Louis Armstrong at Frank Sebastian's New Cotton Club in Los Angeles and, on October 16th of that same year, Hampton made his recording début on vibraphone with the Louis Armstrong Orchestra, featuring a celebrated solo on 'Memories of You'.

By 1934, Lionel Hampton was leading his own band at the Cotton Club and it was then that Benny Goodman first heard him on vibraphone and invited him to augment the trio he had with Teddy Wilson and Gene Krupa. Hamp's spell with Goodman lasted from 1936 to 1940, when Lionel formed his first big band and, with his enormous energy and extravagant showmanship, began touring the globe and taking the jazz world by storm.

Over the years, the Hampton band featured a dazzling array of soloists. Saxophonists, in addition to Johnny Griffin, included Vido Musso, Chu Berry, Ben Webster, Coleman

Left to right: Johnny Griffin, Arnett Cobb, Lionel Hampton and Herbie Fields, New York's Strand Theater, 1945.

Hawkins, Dexter Gordon, Illinois Jacquet, Arnett Cobb, Morris Lane, Teo Macero, Corky Corcoran and Frank Foster. Among the trumpet stars were Ziggy Elman, Henry 'Red' Allen, Ernie Royal, Snooky Young, Clark Terry, Fats Navarro, Jimmy Nottingham, Dizzy Gillespie, Joe Newman, Joe Wilder, Kenny Dorham, Benny Bailey, Idrees Sulieman, Clifford Brown, Cat Anderson, Quincy Jones, Art Farmer and Nat Adderley. And trombonists included Jimmy Cleveland, Al Grey, Lawrence Brown, Britt Woodman and Benny Powell.

'When I joined the Hampton band,' says Griffin, 'the line-up included Joe Morris, Jimmy Nottingham, 'Booty' Wood, Arnett Cobb, Charlie Fowlkes, Milt Buckner, Billy Mackel and Dinah Washington. What a band that was! You really had to work. And it was terrible on drummers. Killed them. They didn't use sticks. They played with small trees. Those pounding drums – I'm sure that's why I can't hear so well in one ear today.

'Sometimes there'd be as many as twelve brass. And there was one trombone section which consisted of one hundred per cent hard drinkers. I got stoned on the fumes from those horns. Phew! They were all my drinking buddies. Sometimes I had to take the trombones apart and wash the snakes out of the slides. The trombones would blow a chord and the saxophone section would pass out.'

After the one-week engagement at the Regal Theater, the Lionel Hampton band, with its new, seventeen-year-old alto saxophonist, left Chicago to go to Toledo, Ohio, for a date at the RKO Theater. It was at that theatre that Johnny Griffin had his first encounter with Hampton's wife and manager, Gladys.

Gladys and Lionel first met in 1929 and were married in Yuma, Arizona, in 1936. That same year, Gladys gave up her own career, as a seamstress in a film studio, to become Lionel Hampton's full-time manager. She was a major influence on his career, helped him organize his first bands and gave him tremendous moral support and encouragement. Hampton once said of Gladys:

'From the time I met her in 1929, she made all the major decisions for me. She was the businesswoman and I was the musician. She was the boss offstage, I was the boss onstage.'

And reflecting on his first meeting with Gladys many years later, Griffin said that, without her, Hamp would have been zero. 'I always liked Gladys – but she got blamed for everything that went wrong.'

When Johnny Griffin walked onto the RKO Theater stage for the sound check, carrying his alto saxophone, he was stopped by Gladys, who said to him, 'Hey, junior, where is your tenor saxophone? What are you doing with that alto?'

Johnny, nonplussed, answered, 'What do you mean, tenor saxophone?'

Said Gladys, 'You're playing tenor in the band.'

And that was the first time that anyone had mentioned to Griffin that he was being hired as a tenor saxophonist. But, needless to say, he was not too dismayed. He had been playing alto like a tenor anyway, growling on it Ben Webster style or trying to emulate Lester Young's sound.

Johnny recalls, 'I needed to get hold of a tenor saxophone fast. There were no instruments to be found in Toledo. So I took a train back to Chicago, found an old Conn tenor and rejoined the band. I had always assumed that I'd been hired as a replacement for Jay Peters, but it turned out that tenor saxophonist Fred Simon had left the band early in 1945 and I was to take his place. Hamp wanted me to do a two-tenor feature on 'Flying Home' with Arnett Cobb.'

Arnett Cleophus Cobb, from Houston, Texas, had joined the Hampton band in 1942, following the departure of Illinois Jacquet. He was dubbed 'the wild man of the tenor saxophone'.

'Arnett had a big, big sound,' remembers Griffin. 'Hamp had lots of these guys from Texas in the band, with loads of experience, so it took me a couple of months to get my sound together and to feel confident enough to compete with Arnett. They used to call us Big Red and Little Red, because we both had a relatively light skin colour. Cobb weighed 230 pounds and I weighed 95, in my overcoat. Soaking wet. At four feet ten, I was even shorter than Milt Buckner – and I didn't think anyone could be shorter than him.'

Griff made his first sides with Hamp for MCA on December 1st 1945 – 'Slide, Hamp, Slide' and 'Hey-ba-ba-re-bop'. He recalls, 'It was good working with the band. They were a great bunch of musicians, but I couldn't stand too much of 'Flying Home'.'

In a *Down Beat* interview with Don Gold, Johnny said that everything Hampton did turned into 'Flying Home'. 'He had a fabulous library and we'd rehearse an extensive selection of tunes, by some of New York's best arrangers, but we'd never play them. Lionel would always wind up playing 'Hamp's Boogie Woogie', 'Hey-ba-ba-re-bop' and 'Flying Home'.'

At this time, says Griffin, his playing was a mixture of Ben Webster, Charlie Parker and Johnny Hodges. But he had now become a devout Don Byas enthusiast.

Byas, from Muskogee, where he was born on October 21st 1912, was a fluent, distinctive and enterprising saxophonist, whose style was part swing and part bop. Johnny once described him as 'the Art Tatum of the saxophone', and he told Art Taylor in his December 1969 interview for Taylor's book, *Notes And Tones*:

'Until I spoke to Don recently, I didn't know how close he had been with Tatum. As a kid coming up, I could hear something in it. Now, twenty years later, I find out that Don was around Tatum and he was using his harmonic solutions.'[4]

Don Byas came to Europe in September 1946 with the Don Redman Orchestra for a tour organized by the Danish journalist, concert and record producer and broadcaster, Timme Rosenkrantz. Redman's was the first non-military American ensemble to perform in Europe after the Second World War.

At the end of that tour, Byas decided to settle in Europe, living first in Paris and then moving, in 1955, to Amsterdam, where, like Johnny Griffin, he married a Dutch woman.

I interviewed Don Byas for the *Melody Maker* in July 1967 and he had much the same outlook on the jazz scene of that time as did Griffin, describing free jazz as 'murder' and saying that it disgusted him. He also said, (shades of Griff):

'I was one of the instigators of bop because I could play so fast.'

He added that he had always been an originator, never an imitator. Hawk was his great idol initially, but he never tried to copy him. Again like Griffin, Byas said his main inspiration came from pianists – in particular, Art Tatum. 'He was a genius and the jazz world really suffered when he died. I played with Tatum quite a bit, but I never made any records with him.'

In the mid-1940s, Griffin was also listening to Charlie Parker, Dizzy Gillespie and Fats Navarro. Altogether, Griffin saw Bird play on about ten occasions. 'I was completely overawed by the man,' he says. 'He showed not only the potential of the saxophone, but the potential of human expression. At times, Bud Powell was like this, too.'

Griffin was completely fascinated by the new music, which he dearly wanted to play, but he felt that he could not assimilate it while sitting on the bandstand playing 'Air Mail Special' and 'Hey-ba-ba-re-bop' year-in, year-out. It was clear that the musical times were changing. Says Johnny: 'Hamp was always telling me, "You're the greatest, you're the greatest," but I really wanted to move on and get into this exciting new music.'

When Griffin was in New York with the Hampton band in January 1946, he went to 52nd Street to listen to Coleman Hawkins, whom he had met in Chicago in the early 1940s. 'But,' Johnny recalls, 'I was seventeen years old and the man on the door wouldn't let me in.' But then Coleman Hawkins came over and told the doorman to let Griffin enter. 'He plays with Hamp's band,' said Bean. After the Hawkins set, Johnny Griffin would go to the club next door to catch the Dizzy Gillespie group, which included Milt Jackson and Ray Brown.

When the Hampton band was in New York, Griffin would stay at the Braddock Hotel, which was located west of the Apollo Theater in Harlem. It was much frequented by jazz musicians, including Jo Jones and other members of the Basie band, and many Duke Ellington sidemen. Dizzy Gillespie, Dinah Washington, Billie Holiday and Billy Eckstine were also regular guests. Musicians appearing at the Apollo would go to the Braddock Hotel bar between sets and Griffin remembers that he spent most of his time in that bar.

In New York, the Hampton band would play a six-week engagement at the Strand Theater on Broadway, doing four shows a day, and, twice a year, the band would play a week at the Apollo Theater. 'New York was really jumping in those days,' says Griffin. But his growing enthusiasm for the revolutionary new music that was being pioneered by Charlie Parker, Dizzy Gillespie, Fats Navarro and by Kenny Clarke, Thelonious Monk, Charlie Christian and other denizens of Minton's Playhouse on Harlem's 118th Street, made a departure from the Lionel Hampton band inevitable.

A fleeting reflection of the early stages of Griffin's conversion to bebop can be heard in his solo on 'Tempo's Birthday', which the Hampton band recorded on September 9th 1946. As Alain Gerber observes in his liner note to the MCA LP, *Slide, Hamp, Slide*, which contained this track, 'Johnny Griffin was at the dawn of his career and was tentatively following in the footsteps of Charlie Parker, notably in the concluding notes of his solo.'

Trumpeter Joe Morris shared Griffin's frustration – and together they decided to quit Hampton and form their own small group. Morris had been with Hampton since 1942 and had contributed some originals to the book, including 'Chop Chop', 'Tempo's Birthday' and 'Punch And Judy'. He also wrote the arrangement of vocalist Dinah Washington's first big hit, 'Evil Gal Blues', a Leonard Feather composition which Dinah recorded with a small group from the Hampton band in December 1943.

Morris left the Hampton band in the summer of 1946 and was followed by Johnny Griffin in December of that year. Griffin went back to Chicago, where he and Morris formed a group with local musicians: baritone saxophonist Bill McLemore, guitarist George Freeman, pianist Wilmus Reeves, bassist Embra Daylie and drummer Leroy Jackson. It was essentially a rhythm and blues outfit, although Griffin really wanted the band to head in the bebop direction.

However, when Arnett Cobb quit the Hampton band in March 1947 to form his own group, Lionel Hampton contacted Johnny and asked him to rejoin the band. Griffin accepted the offer and was given a seven-year contract – but he stayed for just two months. He quit in May 1947 and rejoined Joe Morris and the septet, having, he said, 'played 'Flying Home' and 'Hamp's Boogie Woogie' 73,519 times. I just got tired of playing the same tunes. It was just too much for me.

'Working with Hamp was a tremendous experience, but he was a poor payer. When I joined the band in 1945, I was making $118 a week, and so was Dinah Washington. And yet I was a featured soloist and Dinah had had a really big hit with 'Evil Gal Blues' in 1944. Hamp, on the other hand, was making a pile of money. They said that Gladys was responsible for the low pay, but, after her death in 1977, Hamp continued to pay lousy wages, although he was making so much money. He preferred to pay the musicians low wages and have them dependent, rather than pay them good money and let them live well.'

4

To Be or Not to Bop?

The Johnny Griffin–Joe Morris Septet recorded a number of sides for the Manor, Saxophonograph, Aladdin and Atlantic labels between late-1946 and November 1949. The band also recorded three numbers with singer Wynonie Harris in Linden, New Jersey, in April 1949.

Recalling his time with Joe Morris, Johnny Griffin says, 'When the band started, we were playing a few bebop numbers but they were done in R&B style. The repertoire was primarily rhythm and blues and boogie. We got hooked up with two men from Washington, DC, who had dreams of starting a new record label.'

That new label was Atlantic Records, which was founded in October 1947, and the Joe Morris Band was one of its first signings. The president of the company, Herb Abramson, had been a jazz promoter and part-time a&r man for National Records, who had been producing such artists as Billy Eckstine and Pete Johnson. Ahmet Ertegun, the co-founder and vice president, was a passionate jazz enthusiast and record collector. Abramson's wife, Miriam, was vice president in charge of administration and took care of the accounting.

Atlantic had rather cramped offices in New York's Jefferson Hotel. The company built its early reputation with R&B repertoire by Joe Turner and Ruth Brown – and, later, recordings by LaVern Baker, the Drifters, the Coasters and Ray Charles. Atlantic established a reputation for integrity, treating its artists with respect and paying royalties of between three and five per cent, whereas it was the normal industry practice to pay royalties below two per cent and very often, in the case of black artists, no royalties whatsoever.

A compilation CD, released by France's Classics Records in 2003, features twenty-six tracks by the Morris/Griffin group that were originally recorded for the Atlantic label. And ironically, given the two leaders' chronic frustration at having to play the same numbers every night with Lionel Hampton, the opening track of the album – a Morris composition called 'Fly, Mister, Fly' – is a pastiche of 'Flying Home', complete with the same Hampton riff passage in the final bridge.

The Classics compilation, titled *Joe Morris 1946–1949*, provides a vivid illustration of a band in the process of metamorphosing from a rhythm and blues outfit to a bebop group. First of all, it has to be said that the performances are, for the most part, somewhat rough and ready, often turgid and, occasionally, downright sluggish. But it is the sound of a seven-piece group being pulled in two different directions that makes this album so fascinating.

Johnny Griffin, who was eighteen when the first six of these sides were recorded, was already introducing improbable quotes into his solos. On three of the numbers, including – unavoidably – 'Weasel Walk', he inserts a phrase from 'Pop Goes the Weasel', and other solos are adorned with snatches of 'I'm a Yankee Doodle Dandy', 'Louise', 'Chicago' and 'Jumping with Symphony Sid'. Griffin's playing on these sessions often echoes that of his future Tough Tenors partner, Eddie 'Lockjaw' Davis.

According to the CD booklet, eighteen of the twenty-six numbers were written by Joe Morris, with Griff contributing 'The Spider', and co-writing 'Tia Juana' with Morris and 'Jax Boogie' with Morris and Bill McLemore. But one composition attributed to Morris, 'Beans and Cornbread', had actually been written by Fred Clark and Fleecie Moore and was a hit for Louis Jordan who recorded it in June 1947.

Morris was clearly keen to move into Louis Jordan territory because tracks such as 'Joe's Boogie' and 'Boogie Woogie Joe' are very much in the Jordan mode. But he also ventures into Dizzy-land with a boppish vocal on 'Wow' (not to be confused with the Lennie Tristano original of the same name, which was recorded some months later, in May 1949). 'The Spider', a thirty-two-bar theme, is a feature for Griffin, who plays with a far rougher, more guttural tone than usual, emulating Arnett Cobb and punctuating his solos with uncharacteristic honks and screeches and repeated motor car horn effects. Yet there are some boppish moments on the bridge and Griff signs off with a flattened fifth note. On 'Wilma's Idea', another piece with bop phrases, Griffin's solo combines elements of Arnett Cobb and Charlie Parker, but on numbers such as 'Mad Moon', 'Easy Riff', 'Weasel Walk' and 'Boogie Woogie March', he adopts a coarse, strident tone and laces his solos with more honks and screeches. 'Out of the Night', a boppish Morris original in the key of F, has Griffin soloing in a more familiar style and the theme ends on a B natural – the flattened fifth. And, in another nod in the direction of the beboppers, the bridge of 'Jump With Me' includes a quote from Dizzy Gillespie's 'Salt Peanuts', which Dizzy first recorded with Charlie Parker in May 1945. Cobb's influence on Griffin is very much in evidence on 'Bam-a-Lam-a-Lam', a Morris original which might have come straight out of the Lionel Hampton book.

It was in 1948, on a tour with the Morris band – which included pianist Elmo Hope, bassist Bobby Burton and drummer Philly Joe Jones – that Johnny Griffin came face to face with the ugly reality of the racism that polluted the southern states of America. The band played a gig in Montgomery, Alabama and, on the following day, the musicians were invited to a party.

Montgomery, the birthplace of Joe Morris, was not noted for its commitment to civil rights and racial equality. It was in this city, back in February 1861, that Jefferson Davis was inaugurated President of the, then, seven Confederate States of America and Montgomery became the Confederacy's first capital. It was from this city that the telegram ordering the South Carolina Confederates to open fire on Fort Sumner was dispatched, precipitating the American Civil War. Some nine decades later, Montgomery was the scene of another conflict – the battle for civil rights – during which forty people died in the city between 1955 and 1968.

On the way to the party, the band got lost and Johnny Griffin volunteered to go into a nearby police station to ask for directions. Recalling the occasion, Johnny says:

'I had on a beige suit, a pea-green trench coat and a hat to match. When I went into the station, the policemen called out "Nigger!" so many times before I'd even taken five steps. I looked around to see who they were shouting at. Then, one of them said, "You, nigger – come here and take your hat off. You got your hat on in a police station. Are you crazy?" Then they told me to go back out again through a different door. There was a Black Maria outside. They bundled me into it and took me to the local jail. That was the penalty for walking into a police station with my hat on. One of the policemen asked me for my name and then for my mother's name and when I told them, "Mrs. Betty Griffin," he shouted, "Niggers don't have no Mr and Mrs down here!" And every time he said "nigger" I'd flinch.

'They put me in a cell with about twenty-five other guys – some roaring drunk – and all of them black. I was in total shock. There was this big, rough looking black guy sitting in a special space in the corner. It was pretty quiet around him, so I went straight in his direction, with him not taking his eyes off me. I had a joint left in my pocket and I handed it to him, hoping that he smoked. That put a big smile on his face – and he told me to sit down on the bunk next to him. He cleared a space around him. He was my man. He didn't take the joint, so I smoked it myself and then fell asleep.'

When he awoke the next morning, Johnny was taken to the local courthouse, where his irrepressible sense of humour stood him in good stead.

He recalls: 'Funnily enough, the judge didn't have a deep southern accent, though he was probably a local – maybe educated in the north. When I went before him, the clerk announced that I was charged with being drunk. But I hadn't had a drink all day, because I was going to a party. If they'd caught me a couple of hours later, they would have had a case. The judge asked me if I had anything to say and I said, 'Your honour, I was railroaded. I was on my way to a party and I walked into the police station to ask directions. They got angry because I had my hat on. I didn't know that I had to take off my hat in front of men. I take it off in front of women. They called me all kinds of niggers and so – I was railroaded.' People started laughing at that point. The judge said, 'Case dismissed,' and I was out of there.

'When I walked out of the courthouse, I found myself in a big city square which had a statue of Jefferson Davis flourishing the Confederate flag. Very symbolic! I began walking to get as far away as possible from the court and the police – and then I realized I was walking straight into a white area of the city. I didn't see any black people – but happily Philly Joe Jones and Joe Morris arrived on the scene in the band's wagon and picked me up. When I told them what had happened, they just roared with laughter.

'On that same tour, we were in Jacksonville, Florida and I was burning up with thirst, so I went to a drinking fountain. I started to drink – and a woman screamed, because I was drinking at the part of the fountain reserved for white people. There was a lead pipe some distance away, which had the sign *Colored*. But, you see, I'm from Chicago, so I pay no attention to these signs.'

The first edition of the Joe Morris band, assembled in Chicago, lasted for a year or so; then, early in 1948, Morris and Griffin went back to New York and reorganized the group.

'We were looking for a piano player, and it was trumpeter Benny Harris who brought us Elmo Hope. We had Matthew Gee on trombone, Bill McLemore on baritone saxophone, Percy Heath or Nelson Boyd on bass and Philly Joe Jones on drums, and we were playing arrangements of Monk and Bud Powell tunes which were very advanced for their time.'

Elmo Hope was a boyhood friend of Bud Powell. A self-taught pianist, he played in clubs in the Bronx, Coney Island and Greenwich Village and then had a spell with the

orchestra of Lawrence 'Snub' Mosley. Later he worked with
Sonny Rollins, Lou Donaldson, Clifford Brown, Art Blakey,
John Coltrane and Hank Mobley.

'It was through Elmo Hope that I met Thelonious Monk
and Bud Powell,' says Johnny Griffin. 'Those three piano
players were always together. I started hanging out with
them and, happily, they accepted me. I'd learned a little bit
about the keyboard and I was always trying to see what they
were doing, because I didn't want to play like other saxophonists – that's why I hung out with pianists. The piano for
me is the whole orchestra. The time I spent with those three
pianists was my higher education in music. They were my
teachers. From them I learned more about the harmonic
structures underlying the music.

'I met Thelonious in 1948 and spent a lot of time at his
house on 116th Street, with Elmo and Bud. Monk didn't play
much – except when he was rehearsing his own band. He'd sit
there and check out what Elmo and Bud were doing.
Sometimes I'd have my horn out and play, but mostly I'd be
listening.

'They had the vast musical knowledge that I wanted. We
would go from house to house where they always had pianos.
Walter Bishop Jr. was there some of the time – he played like
Bud, but they treated him like a junior. We'd go into their
houses and I'd start banging on the piano, but Bud would
push me off and take over. Then Elmo would play – he
was the only pianist that Bud would allow to play around
him. Monk didn't even play – Bud wouldn't let him. But he
would always play Thelonious' music. It was always music,
music, music, twenty-four hours a day – that was my university education, on the streets of New York and in various

apartments, playing and listening all the time, hanging out with those musicians.

'From 1948 to 1951 I was with those three piano players almost every day. We'd go from 116th Street all the way up to Elmo's house on Kelly Street in the Bronx. Elmo had a similar technique to Bud and he and Bud were very close. I've seen them play together: two pianos – Bach preludes and fugues. I've seen them play Christmas medleys on two pianos up in the Bronx club. Elmo was the only pianist that Bud really wanted to play with – he kind of worshipped Elmo.

'People said that Monk had no technique – but that's crazy. Monk played exactly what he wanted to play – you never heard Monk stumble over anything – ever. It was very definite. I think technique is very overrated, especially today – in jazz anyway. With improvised music, you are playing what comes to you directly, spontaneously – and if your brain is able to interpret the feelings of your heart, you play what you want to play. That's as much technique as you need.

'Bud wasn't too interested in other pianists – except Elmo, Monk and Art Tatum. He had a way of playing which was particularly his own – I called him a thumper – the way he thumped the keys was very percussive. Elmo had a lighter touch, but they had almost the same conception of modern harmony. Bud was more forceful. Elmo had an aggressiveness of his own – but his touch was much lighter, more *legato*. Bud had more power. They both made the same facial grimaces. They looked as if they were going to bite the piano – teeth bared like wild tigers. And the grunting. Everything was done emphatically, everything meant something.

'Bud Powell was the greatest influence on jazz piano from the 1940s on. He had more influence on young pianists coming up playing modern music than any other pianist I know of. Monk had a different influence. But was more pianistically so. Monk scored with composition and effects, special effects, spatial effects. But the swing was still there.

'When Joe Morris and I were working in The Three Deuces, with Philly Joe Jones, Percy Heath and Elmo Hope, Bud and Monk were in the audience. We were playing opposite George Shearing, who had Oscar Pettiford and J. C. Heard in his trio. He had just come over from England.'

Arthur Taylor, in his book *Notes And Tones*, records Griffin telling him: 'I wanted to be original, so I was afraid to hang out with other saxophone players. I spent most of my spare time with pianists. I learned my lessons from Bud Powell, Elmo Hope and Thelonious Monk. Most of my musical knowledge came from them. And from trumpet players Charlie Shavers, Kenny Dorham, Fats Navarro, Clifford Brown and Dizzy Gillespie.

'I used to go with Thelonious when he collected his unemployment pay. I would watch Monk's group rehearsing, but I didn't play with him. They'd rehearse for months, then go to a gig over in Brooklyn and get fired after the first set. "That's not music," the club owner would tell Monk. Ten years later, when I was playing with Monk in the Five Spot in New York, this guy from Brooklyn showed up and he desperately wanted to hire Monk's band, but he just couldn't afford him.'

For Johnny Griffin, the late 1940s meant, in his words, 'hard times and hungry days'. He says, 'There were the odd gigs that would pop up and we didn't starve to death. I made R&B record dates to make ends meet.'

The Morris/Griffin collaboration lasted till the end of 1949, when the band split in two over the question of commercialism. Griffin left the group because Morris wanted to concentrate on rhythm and blues repertoire, while Johnny

CD insert for *Anytime, Anyplace, Anywhere* by Joe Morris and his orchestra, featuring Johnny Griffin and singer Laurie Tate.

was anxious to become involved in the new bebop movement. He says, 'I left Morris because I wanted to blow – and I formed a quartet with Elmo Hope, Gene Ramey on bass and Papa Jo Jones on drums. This was in 1950 and the group lasted for about five months.'

Joe Morris went on to play rhythm and blues, working with singers Laurie Tate, Billy Mitchell, Faye Adams and Ursula Reed. His June 1950 Atlantic recording of 'Anytime, Anyplace, Anywhere', with a vocal by Laurie Tate, reached the number one spot on the *Billboard* rhythm and blues chart.

In 1951 Griffin received an offer from his old Hampton colleague, Arnett Cobb. He wanted Johnny to join his group – not on tenor but on baritone saxophone. Johnny accepted – but remembers having some misgivings: 'Arnett let me play

'These Foolish Things' on tenor once a night, but everything else was on baritone.'

Griffin struggled at first to get a full sound on the baritone saxophone and finally solved the problem when he acquired a good Runyon mouthpiece from Chicago. But when his sound and technique improved, Cobb decided to feature him less. During his time with the Cobb group, Griffin recorded four sides on baritone for the Okeh label with Willie Moore (trumpet), Dickie Harris (trombone), Cobb (tenor saxophone), George Rhodes (piano), Walter Buchanan (bass) and Al Walker (drums).

'But,' Johnny recalls, 'we were doing a gig in Cleveland and we had a run-in. We were playing opposite [guitarist] Tiny Grimes, who had Red Prysock on tenor saxophone and Freddie Redd on piano. One night, Arnett was late arriving at the gig and when Tiny finished his set and it was time for us to play, the club owner asked us to start without Arnett. I said OK and went on stage with my tenor. I called a number that was really fast and furious. I was flying! And when Cobb arrived in the club, he went berserk. At the end of the number he snapped, "How dare you start without me." So I quit. I went back to Chicago – and then the Draft Board caught up with me.'

5

The Life-Saving Oboe

When Johnny Griffin was drafted in 1951, he was posted to
Fort Sheridan, a United States Army camp outside Chicago,
which was named after Civil War Cavalry General, Philip
Sheridan, in recognition of his services to Chicago.

'I went with seven or eight other black cats,' says Johnny.
'When we got to Fort Sheridan, we learned that we were to
be posted to a camp in Arkansas. When we heard that, we
told the lieutenant that we would refuse to go to the segre-
gated South. So, instead, we were sent to do our training in
Hawaii, which we considered to be a much more attractive
proposition – with hula girls, sunshine, the islands. Fantastic!

'We had to do eight weeks of basic training, eight weeks of
advanced training and two weeks of light artillery training –
and then we were to be posted to Korea, where the war had
been raging for two years.'

And, once again – not long after he'd been shipped to
Scofield Barracks in Hawaii en route to the killing fields of
Korea – Johnny Griffin's training under Captain Walter
Dyett at DuSable High School came to his rescue.

He recalls: 'The 45th Regiment combat team trained in
that Hawaii camp and it sustained a casualty rate in Korea of

Griffin's army days 1951–53

seventy-five per cent, killed or wounded. When my battalion graduated, our orders were to go to Korea, which didn't fill me with enthusiasm. It so happened that, at the time of graduation, they put a notice on the bulletin board in the orderly room, which said that anyone with musical talent, who wanted to participate in the entertainment programme at the officers' club, could sign up and be considered.

'Well, I knew some of the musicians in the battalion, so I got them together, rehearsed a few arrangements and auditioned for the programme. We played our buns off at the audition, passed the test, went on to the programme and then proceeded to blow the army dance band off the stage. They were a sad a bunch of cats, anyway. The colonel got very drunk and jumped up and said, "OK. Put that boy, that boy and that boy in the band."

'But first they had to check our records to see that our qualifications, in terms of reading music and so on, were up to scratch. They looked at my records and saw that I had played oboe – and this was exactly what the bandmaster wanted – an oboe player. So they put me in the station band and that saved my life. But the other six guys in the group I'd put together didn't make it. They were posted to Korea and they all got killed in 1951 and 1952, every one of them.'

Griffin was a member of the 264th Army Band in Hawaii for eighteen months. On many evenings during that period, he would be in Honolulu playing jazz gigs. On his discharge from the army in 1953, he returned to Chicago, where he worked with various bands and also led his own groups for four years. In this period he recorded sides, as leader, for Epic, Argo and Blue Note.

* * *

In April 1953, he made his first recordings as leader – four sides for the Okeh company recorded in Chicago and titled *Little Johnny Griffin and his Orchestra*, with Babs Gonzales and a group of other musicians whom the discographies don't list. And, no doubt as a gesture to Hamp, one of the numbers was

'Flying Home', featuring a vocal by Gonzales. Babs, who was a band boy with the Jimmie Lunceford Orchestra in the 1930s, also put a lyric to 'For Dancers Only', a Sy Oliver composition, which Lunceford recorded in 1937. Johnny Griffin had first met Babs Gonzales at the Apollo Theater when he was with Lionel Hampton, and Babs' group, Three

Babs Gonzales

Bips and a Bop, was guesting with the band. Gonzales (real name, Lee Brown), was from Newark, New Jersey, where he was born on October 27th 1919. A pianist and drummer as well as a scat vocalist, Babs worked with Benny Carter, Charlie Barnet and Lionel Hampton in the 1940s. He was best known for the vocal and instrumental quartet, Three Bips and a Bop, which he formed in 1946, with himself as vocalist, Rudy Williams on alto saxophone, Tadd Dameron on piano, Pee Wee Tinney on guitar, Art Phipps on bass, and Charles Simon on drums.

Gonzales was a bebop camp follower who sought to popularize the new music. His group cut a number of sides for the Blue Note and Apollo labels in early 1947, including 'Oop-pop-a-da'. This number was recorded by Dizzy Gillespie in June of that year, but Gonzales never got composer credit. The tune has always been attributed either solely to Gillespie, or to Gillespie and alto saxophonist John Brown, or Gillespie and composer/arranger Gil Fuller.

Possessed of a larger than life personality, Babs Gonzales – to whom Griffin's composition 'Blues for Gonzi' was dedicated – wrote two autobiographical volumes: *I Paid My Dues:*

Good Times . . . No Bread in 1967 and *Movin' On Down De Line* in 1975, published by his own Expubident Publishing Corp. Both volumes were spectacularly misspelt and full of delightful inaccuracies but highly colourful and sporadically amusing.

Gonzales records that, by the time he was thirteen, he was 'hustling newspapers, shining shoes and running errands for whores.' But, he added, he spent most of his time womanising and borrowing money. The books teem with life – mostly the seamier side – including some wry ghetto imagery, and they reflect a deep hostility towards the exploitative whites, which undoubtedly stemmed from Gonzales' ghetto upbringing. He could scarcely be blamed for feeling bitter towards the white supremacists as some of the material in his books illustrates vividly. In *Movin' On Down De Line* Gonzales recalls an occasion in 1968 when he was waiting for a taxi at New York's Penn Station. Three cabs arrived, let their white passengers out, but refused to pick him up. 'After forty minutes,' he writes, 'I jumped in one as soon as the other passengers got out.' When the cabbie protested and shouted at Babs to get out, he told him, 'Drive me to the nearest police station.'

About two blocks from the station, the driver saw two policemen. He jumped out and screamed at the cops that Babs had a knife and was threatening to kill him. 'As usual,' Babs notes, 'I couldn't say anything. It was "All right, nigger, hands over the hood."

'They were very disappointed at not finding any weapon on me or behind the seat.'

All the way to the police station the police insulted Gonzales with crude racist jibes; once there they took all his belongings and locked him in a cell without granting him the obligatory telephone call. They confiscated his shoes and, the next morning, took him, barefoot, to City Hall where they told him that, if he agreed to be fingerprinted, he would be allowed to call his lawyer.

But after taking his prints, the police again denied him the call and put him back in a cell. 'I was in the pen waiting to face the judge when a detective I went to school with saw me. He eased out and called my lawyer. I was in front of the judge with the whole court laughing at my bare feet when she arrived.'

Gonzales was remanded for one week in the custody of his lawyer and was determined to bring an action against the police for wrongful arrest. But his lawyer said to him, 'Yeah, Babs, you got a good case, but I can't make it as my husband works for the City.'

He saw four more lawyers that week, some of whom he had known since childhood, but they all told him the same thing: 'You can't fight City Hall.'

'So,' says Babs, 'I had to pay a fifty dollar fine with no redress, period. I say to all black people who never been in jail: You ain't got *no rights* even if you got bread, if you're black.'

Gonzales' most celebrated record sessions were those he did for Capitol in January, March and April 1949, the best-known titles being 'Capitolizing' and 'Professor Bop', which not only featured Gonzales' special brand of bop vocalese but also marked the recording début of Sonny Rollins.

In the 1950s he worked with J. J. Johnson, Bennie Green, James Moody, Buddy Tate, Clark Terry, Art Pepper and Champion Jack Dupree, and then branched out into record production, artist management and promotion and also worked as a radio disc jockey. As a bop-scat specialist,

Gonzales had a flair for putting lyrics to instrumental bebop solos, including Charlie Parker's 'Ornithology'. He performed regularly in Europe, most frequently in Sweden and France, made $10,000 on a tour of Swedish folk parks and lost every cent in a failed Paris nightclub venture.

Gonzales and Griffin would team up once again – in July 1958 – when they made the album, *Voila*, for the Hope label, with Les Spann (flute), Charlie Rouse (bass clarinet), Horace Parlan (piano), Ray Crawford (guitar), Peck Morrison (bass), Roy Haynes (drums) and Melba Liston as arranger.

In 1975, Babs performed at several European jazz festivals, including Montreux, and also gave concerts in Holland. The latter incorporated a twenty-minute anti-drug lecture. In early 1979 he was in London and sat in a couple of times at the Pizza Express and Ronnie Scott's Club. At that time he was living in Holland, but later that year he returned to the United States. He died of cancer in his home town of Newark on January 23rd 1980.

* * *

On the 1953 Okeh sides with Gonzales, Griffin plays mostly in 'Texas tenor' mode, honking and rasping his way through the first two titles and his own medium tempo B flat blues, 'Chicago Riffin'', but he plays with soul and sensitivity on his ballad 'Till We Meet Again'. And, as ever, he scatters quotes throughout his solos, including 'Mexican Hat Dance', 'Pop Goes the Weasel', 'Buttons and Bows' and Dvorak's 'Humoresque'.

Johnny's return to Chicago in 1953 gave him the opportunity to have a family reunion and also to resume his relationship with a young lady he had first met in 1951, when he played a gig in the Cotton Club, located at 6249 Cottage

Grove. Her name was Joan Ross and she was the manager of the club. Some months after their first meeting, Joan and Johnny began going out together and, on August 24th 1954, they were married at the interdenominational Metropolitan Community Church on the South Side.

At this time, Johnny was gigging around his home city; 'I had offers to come back to New York but I was doing OK in Chicago. I was working in the Blue Note there, opposite Ella, with George Freeman, Wilbur Ware and Wilbur Campbell. Babs Gonzales came to Chicago and he worked with us.

'Once in a while I did gigs with Gene Ammons and Lester Young. I loved Prez – he was a nice, quiet person and always positive – and so cute with that hat on the back of his head, those big pop eyes and his special way of talking – "Lady Griffin, I don't know what I am going to do with you," he would say and he would usually speak of himself in the third person.'

For a short time Johnny led a sextet at the Regal Theater and, as he recalled in his 1993 *Cadence* interview with Alwyn and Laurie Lewis, musicians from Detroit would come to Chicago and try to take over the gig scene. One night, Johnny had a tenor battle on stage with Billy Mitchell, who had come to Chicago from Detroit with a bop group. Griffin played a solo and then Mitchell followed and this went on for about forty-five minutes. Then Billy Mitchell looked at Griffin and said, 'All right – we'll split the city. You can take half and I'll take the other half.'

Chicago was a hive of jazz activity in the 1950s, as Nathan Davis recalled when I interviewed him in January 2007:

'It was in Chicago that I met Johnny Griffin for the first time. This was in 1955 and I had travelled to Chicago by overnight bus from Kansas City to continue my studies – first at Crane Tech and then, for one summer, at DuSable High School.

'The city boasted some superb musicians, quite a number of whom never received the recognition they deserved – such as tenor saxophonist Nicky Hill and guitarist Reginald Boyd. It was predominantly a saxophone stronghold and, without question, Johnny Griffin was the boss tenor man.

'I was staying with an aunt and uncle and, one Monday morning, my uncle took me to the Flame Show Lounge on 39th Street where they had what were known as Blue Monday jam sessions, which started at seven or eight in the morning after the cats had been playing all night. This place was a tenor saxophone heaven. On stage that morning were Griff, Ira Sullivan – playing just like Sonny Stitt – Nicky Hill, John Gilmore, Eddie Harris and Clifford Jordan. I think Jodie Christian was on piano, Wilbur Ware on bass and Wilbur Campbell was one of the drummers.

'I had my saxophone with me, hoping to get to sit in. But when I opened the door, I heard a hail of machine gun bullet notes. It scared the hell out of me – so I shut the door right quick. After a while I plucked up courage and went in. The guys were playing this wild up-tempo piece, which went on for about an hour. In the course of one session they'd get through three or four different drummers.

'I sat there until they finished the set and finally steeled myself to get up onstage and play with that incredible saxophone sextet. After that introduction, I would regularly skip class on Mondays and head for the Flame Show Lounge.

'During the year I spent in Chicago, Johnny Griffin became my hero. He made one hell of an impression on me.

A late 1950s session at Chicago's Gate of Horn, organized by Joe Segal, with *left to right*: singer Oscar Brown Jr., pianist Jodie Christian, Griffin, bassist Bill Lee, drummer Marshall Thompson (hidden) and Frank London Brown who was regularly featured presenting his fictional 'Readings in Jazz' with improvised music (photo Joe Segal).

He had his own special sound and, when it came to jam sessions, he was a phenomenal ass-kicker!'

Johnny recalls that when Sonny Stitt came to Chicago he would drive all the saxophone players crazy. 'He knew every hip bebop cliché. When I was in New York, he would come to my hotel room and ask me to play something on the tenor. I would play a few phrases on the saxophone and he'd say, "OK, give me your horn." Then he would play it and make me feel like I didn't know a damn thing about anything. Things like that would drive me into a corner. But, for all that, I loved the guy.

'It took me years before I felt I could invite him up on the bandstand without being humiliated. I'd go into a corner and practise for hours and hours and would be learning all the time while running around with Elmo, Bud and Monk and listening to them playing. There was no competitive element involved with them; but any time you played with Sonny Stitt, it would be automatic competition.

'I played with Wardell Gray and Dexter and it was beautiful – no competition, just fun. But with Stitt it was a pitched battle from the word go – because that was his thing. He was a great musician, but so arrogant. He would have made a hell of a teacher. But, later on, I appreciated those contests because Sonny really made me learn how to play. He just made me go and learn. Not that I wanted to play like him. I never wanted to play like anybody. But I would use everybody's vocabulary to get out of it what I wanted.

Griffin's first album for Blue Note *Chicago Calling – Introducing Johnny Griffin*, 1956.

'I remember the first gig Sonny Stitt and I did together at the Bee Hive in Chicago. The other musicians were asking, somewhat incredulously, "Are you going to play with Sonny Stitt?" I told them, "That's right." The people in the club were eager to see this duel. So we get on the bandstand and Sonny plays the first solo on tenor. When he's finished, I come right behind him and play my solo. He puts his tenor down, picks up his alto and plays another solo – after which, I play another tenor solo. He says, "You already had a solo." And I say, "Yes, but you also played two solos. And I don't have an alto, so I had to play both solos on tenor – but what I played in the second solo was different from what I played in the first solo."

'I knew that if I could make a mess of his continuity, I'd got him, because he was a perfectionist with everything he did. His clichés were impeccably played, from beginning to end. But what I found out was that he knew what he was going to play before he hit the bandstand. No spontaneity. So I got so I could memorize his solos and knew what he was going to play – then I could spend my time disturbing his continuity.

'Sonny Stitt really made me learn how to play fast and think fast. I guess I've always had a yen to play really fast. I picked that up when I first heard Charlie Parker's 'Ko-ko' – which he'd recorded with Miles, Dizzy and Max Roach in November 1945. That was a music lesson – I could listen to it a thousand times a day. Then I heard Don Byas with Slam Stewart at Town Hall and I thought, "Oh my God!" The fluidity!'

In 1956, Johnny Griffin recorded the album *J. G.* for Argo, with Junior Mance, Wilbur Ware and Buddy Smith. He followed this, in April of the same year, with his first Blue Note

LP, *Chicago Calling – Introducing Johnny Griffin*, which he recorded in Rudy Van Gelder's Hackensack Studio with Wynton Kelly, Curley Russell and Max Roach. At this time, he was leading his quartet at Chicago's Flame Show Lounge. His performance of the high-speed 'Mil Dew' on this album is breathtaking.

The following year, Johnny Griffin left Chicago and headed for New York where he was to join Art Blakey's Jazz Messengers.

6

Griff Gets a Kick Out of Bu

Art Blakey is such an important figure in jazz and in Johnny Griffin's career, especially on record, that he deserves a detailed portrait. Blakey's contribution to jazz music in the course of a career spanning almost sixty years was prodigious and multi-faceted. He was a ferociously swinging, hugely resourceful and supremely catalytic drummer. He was also an indefatigable champion of the music he loved and an unremitting international campaigner in its cause. He led, for thirty-six years – from 1954 until 1990 – the most vital, dynamic and enduring small group in jazz, the Jazz Messengers. Over the years, as British writer/musician Brian Priestley has observed, the sound of the Jazz Messengers became the virtual definition of the style known as hard bop and was the inspiration for hundreds of similarly orientated combos all over the world.

In addition, Blakey did more than anyone else in jazz to foster emerging talent. More than a hundred musicians graduated from the Art Blakey college of musical education, founded in February 1954 and given the title of Jazz

Messengers by its original pianist and musical director, Horace Silver. Although, as Art would frequently say, 'I don't discover them, they discover me,' the fact is that every musician who joined the Jazz Messengers emerged from the experience a better player.

When Blakey died on October 16th 1990 – just five days after his seventy-first birthday – former Messenger Jackie McLean observed: 'The school is closed for good.' It marked the end of an illustrious and tremendously colourful chapter in jazz history.

Over the years the musicians came and went, but the message remained pretty much the same. Despite the many changes of personnel and instrumentation, the Jazz Messengers group always preserved its fundamental identity and integrity – the constant element in its epic history being, of course, its founding father, Arthur Blakey. He told me back in 1977 when I interviewed him for *Jazz Journal International*:

'It's just that the musicians do things my way. It's my band and my music. I've been up there directing traffic all these years. Right from the beginning, when we formed the first Messengers, they all insisted that I be the leader. I never wanted to be – I just wanted to be a good sideman and have no headaches. But I was more experienced in life than the rest of the guys.'

Blakey's experience in life up to that point had been somewhat less than idyllic. His mother died six months after he was born and he was brought up by one of her cousins.

It has to be said that he was inclined to succumb to a temptation to improvise on the truth when recounting his life story – sometimes, as some of his close associates have told me, he was prone to add a little extra colour to his recollections. But there is absolutely no doubt that his early life was one of severe deprivation.

'My father never contributed a cent to my support,' Art once told me. 'He left my mother sitting in the carriage outside the church and the next time he saw her she was a corpse. She died of a broken heart. My father wouldn't accept me into the family because they were mulattos and I was a nigger. So we had segregation within segregation.'

Blakey was thirteen before he found out that the woman who had raised him was not his natural mother. He said later: 'Finding this out just tore me apart. I didn't say anything. I just split.' He was married at fourteen, became a father just a few months later and a narcotics user before he was out of his teens – a practice that led eventually to his turning on to heroin in the mid-1940s. He finally conquered his heroin addiction in 1963.

He told me in 1977: 'Dope has been around for centuries and when the pressures and tensions of our society get too much, and people are caught at a weak point, they look for an escape. When I first took drugs, I was a young man and I was married to a young woman I was very much in love with. She was trying to finish law school and she was all set to pass her exams – then she had a cerebral hemorrhage and died. I couldn't believe it. I'm running down the street with her dead body in my arms. I'd never even smoked a cigarette up to that point – but when that happened, I went the full route.

'People don't understand some of the things you go through. I live in New York and when I step out on the street it's like being on a battlefield. Also, I'm a second-class citizen – and that means I'm nothing. For all that the black revolutionaries have done, the situation is worse than it ever was.

The Black Power thing set Harlem back sixty years. The blacks could do nothing but tear up their own neighbourhood and begin to kill each other.

'Then all the drugs came in – but it wasn't the blacks that brought them in. And now it seems the blacks have all gone sound asleep. They talk about America being a democracy, but you can't have democracy without equality, without socialism. For all the presidents we've had who are supposed to have been so great, there hasn't been one who has had enough guts to stand up and give us our freedom.

'Every time I come back into the USA and I'm asked by the Customs if I have anything to declare, I say, "No, sir. Nothing to declare but our freedom – and it is forfeited."'

But despite his bitter criticism of persistent racial inequality in the United States, Blakey always remained a staunch champion of his country – 'because it's my country and I want to protect it and help straighten it out. Musicians like Donald Byrd and Lou Donaldson, who became very rich after they left the Messengers, couldn't have done it anywhere else but in America. Guys put the country down, but if there had been no America, there would be no jazz and God knows where we would all have been.'

Most of the record books give the date of Blakey's birth in the industrial city of Pittsburgh as October 11th 1919, but it is quite possible that it was some years earlier than that. Recalling the humble beginnings of his career as a musician, Blakey said: 'When I was thirteen, I was working in the coal mines in Pittsburgh. I also worked in the steel mills. I was already a man. And at fifteen, I had a family. But I wanted a break from dirty and dangerous work, so I got a job playing piano in a small group at the Ritz Club. I was working as a musician at night and trying to finish high school during the day. It was a hard life but it probably made me the person I am today.

'I really wasn't no piano player – I could play a little bit, entirely by ear. But then one day Erroll Garner came into the club while we were rehearsing. He sat in on piano – and that was the end of my piano-playing days. The owner of the club was a real gangster who always carried a big pistol. When he heard Erroll play, he told me to switch to drums and I didn't see any future in arguing with a man who was carrying a gun.

'I never studied the drums. I'm self-educated in just about everything in life. I did it because I had to survive. And I had a bad habit of liking to eat.

'I took my inspiration from Chick Webb and Big Sid Catlett, and I also had a great respect for Ray Bauduc. But the main man was, of course, the boss himself – Kenny Clarke. When I came to New York in 1942, he helped me a lot. You see these drummers today, playing those elaborate kits – that's just for show. Most drummers I know can't get past the snare drum. Kenny Clarke could sit down and play just the snare drum and make a fool out of each one of those show drummers.

'One of the most important things in playing drums is using dynamics. A lot of young drummers today don't use dynamics; yet they are vital, and they've always been an important part of the Messengers' music. The drums are a sensitive instrument and should be played with sensitivity.'

After spells in the bands of Mary Lou Williams (1942) and Fletcher Henderson (1943–44), Blakey became a founder member of the legendary Billy Eckstine band, which included at various times Gene Ammons, Sonny Criss, Tadd Dameron, Miles Davis, Kenny Dorham, Dizzy Gillespie, Dexter Gordon, Wardell Gray, Budd Johnson, Fats Navarro,

Charlie Parker, Leo Parker, Cecil Payne, Sonny Stitt, Lucky Thompson, Sarah Vaughan, Frank Wess and Trummy Young. It was soon after the Eckstine band broke up in 1947, that Blakey decided to make a visit to Africa. He made the trip not, as some writers reported, to study African drumming but to learn about Islamic culture – as he told *Down Beat*'s Herb Nolan in November 1979:

'I went because there wasn't anything else for me to do. I couldn't get any gigs and I had to work my way over on a boat. I went over there to study religion and philosophy. I didn't bother with drums.'

The African experience ultimately led to Blakey's conversion to Islam and the adoption of the name Abdullah Ibn Buhaina.

After his return from Africa, Blakey worked briefly with Lucky Millinder and Buddy DeFranco and, in December 1947, he made his recording début as leader for the Blue Note label. The album, *New Sounds*, featured Blakey with Kenny Dorham (trumpet), Howard Bowe (trombone), Sahib Shihab (alto saxophone), Musa Kaleem – also known as Orlando Wright – (tenor saxophone), Ernie Thompson (baritone saxophone), Walter Bishop Jr. (piano) and Laverne Baker (bass).

In 1949, Blakey assembled a big band which he called the Seventeen Messengers and which included Sonny Rollins and Bud Powell. The band played a number of gigs around New York but it was not economically viable and broke up after a few months.

The prototype group of the Jazz Messengers emerged in February 1954, when Blakey took a quintet into the Birdland club on New York's 52nd Street. He told Herb Nolan: 'I went into Birdland with Clifford Brown, Horace Silver, Curley Russell and Lou Donaldson for a few weeks. We made some live, unrehearsed records (the two-LP Blue Note set, *A Night at Birdland with the Art Blakey Quintet*) and they did pretty well. After that it was Horace who said we should organize a group. He said, "We'll call it the Jazz Messengers." So it was Horace who really put the name on it, and it stuck.'

The Jazz Messengers officially came into being – according to Leonard Feather – in February 1955, when a quintet consisting of Blakey, Kenny Dorham, Hank Mobley, Horace Silver and Doug Watkins played the Blue Note club in Philadelphia. Nine months later the same group was booked in the Café Bohemia in Greenwich Village where it recorded a double LP set for Blue Note (*The Jazz Messengers at the Café Bohemia*) – the first of what was to become a vast collection of Jazz Messengers recordings.

'We started the Messengers,' Blakey recalled, 'because somebody had to mind the store for jazz. No America – no jazz. It is the only culture that America has brought forth. Everything else comes from another continent. It so happens that jazz comes from the black people – and they should know about it, but they know less about it than anybody in the world.'

Throughout his life, Blakey never missed an opportunity to tell his audiences to support the music and he always kept faith with the musical principles with which the Jazz Messengers became universally identified.

He was always totally unimpressed by criticism that his music changed very little stylistically over the years. He steadfastly refused to follow the sixties' jazz exodus into the no-man's-land of soul-funk-crossover-fusion because he was a passionate believer in the straight-ahead, uncompromising, hard-swinging jazz message that he had been putting across since he first started leading his own band.

'I guess I'm hard-headed,' he told me. 'I make my own decisions and try to stick to my principles. I've never made much money from what I do; but I have self-respect and integrity – and we're still managing to please the people.

'When people come in to relax and enjoy themselves after a hard day's work, it is my job to make them happy – to wash away the dust of everyday life. That's what jazz music is all about.'

'Tough love' was the way Bobby Watson felicitously described Blakey's attitude to his musicians. Because Blakey was a man who combined toughness with compassion, realism with sentimentality.

A diabetic, he was tough enough to inject insulin into his body through his sweater while sitting in the band bus without blinking an eyelid. And he was compassionate enough to help musicians financially when they were down on their luck – even though, for most of his life, Blakey was far from rich. He was tough enough to take on tour after gruelling tour, accommodating himself to life on the road with an energy and resilience that a man half his age would have been proud of.

A genuinely humble man, Blakey nevertheless asserted his status as leader in such matters as flying first class while the sidemen went tourist. He would always say that travelling separately from the musicians gave them a chance to talk about him behind his back and relieve their frustrations.

But his humility would show itself on such occasions as when a hard-pressed road manager, late for a plane connection, would be trying, single-handed, to transfer the instruments and baggage from the hotel lobby to the band bus. Blakey would pitch in, load himself up with cases and roar at his musicians to do the same.

His sentimentality was vividly in evidence when, during a European tour in 1988, word reached him that someone had maltreated his pet dog, Half Note. Blakey took the next plane back to New York, sacrificing a couple of dates out of concern for his pet's welfare.

He also had a tremendous affection for children. It was perhaps the hard life and deprivation that he suffered as a child that helped to make him such a sensitive and sympathetic person where children were concerned. He loved kids and was deeply concerned to protect their innocence. He had at least seven of his own and adopted seven more.

He told *Down Beat*'s Kevin Whitehead in a December 1988 interview:

'I look at a kid, he loves me and I fall in love with him. I'll adopt him. Can't afford it? Can't afford not to, 'cause he needs a parent . . . I guess that's something psychological because I was an orphan; I was always by myself. I had nothing to reach back for.'

And, as well as a love of children, Blakey also had a pronounced fondness for ladies. At the age of seventy he could still exercise his roguish charm to considerable effect. On tour in Tbilisi, Georgia, in 1989, he made a very determined play for a young woman who must have been at least fifty years his junior. And when ladies he propositioned would point out that they were married, he would say to them with a wide-eyed, innocent grin, 'Well, you don't have to tell your husband.'

But, of course, the abiding inspiration of Art Blakey's life, his *raison d'être*, was jazz music – the art form he promoted with such diligence, energy and commitment throughout his career. Music was unquestionably the primary source of Blakey's remarkable serenity. He would say:

'There are musicians who used to be in my band who could buy and sell me today; but I can always pick up the phone and call them to come back into the band and, if they are not too busy, they'll drop everything to play with the Messengers. I really appreciate that. You see, the great musicians who have been through the band were people I picked not only for their musicianship and technique but also for their spiritual attitudes, their feeling and their thinking towards music.'

Johnny Griffin was among the ex-Messengers who returned for reunion recordings and concerts in the band's last decade, as well as Walter Davis Jr., Curtis Fuller, Benny Golson, Bill Hardman, Freddie Hubbard, Cedar Walton, Buster Williams and Reggie Workman.

Griffin first met Art Blakey in 1945 and remembers: 'He was in the Billy Eckstine Band at that time and I had seen him with that band when it played Chicago in 1944. That outfit really shook up the jazz world, featuring, at various times, Bird, Dizzy, Dexter, Stitt, Navarro, Miles, Gene Ammons, Leo Parker, Tommy Potter and many more.

'I was in Los Angeles in 1945 and somebody asked me to play this jam session at Billy Berg's Swing Club in Hollywood. Art Blakey was the drummer and that was the start of a life-long friendship. When I came out of the army in 1953, he had Wilbur Ware and Horace Silver in his group and he tried to get me to join him. But I had just gotten home and gotten married, so I said no.'

* * *

It was on March 13th 1957, before he left Chicago to settle in New York, that Johnny made his first recording with Art Blakey in New York's Webster Hall for RCA's Vik label – the somewhat improbable *Selections from Lerner and Loewe's My*

Fair Lady, Brigadoon and Paint Your Wagon, with Bill Hardman
(trumpet), Jackie McLean (alto saxophone), Sam Dockery
(piano) and Spanky De Brest (bass).

'In the course of that session,' says Johnny, 'Blakey asked
me again to join his group as a replacement for Jackie
McLean – so I did.' Thus began a seven-month spell with the
Jazz Messengers.

'When, after a decade in the limbo of pick-up groups and
rhythm-and-blues outfits,' wrote Michael James in the liner
notes to Griffin's March 1967 album, *You Leave Me Breathless*,
'Johnny Griffin came east from Chicago in 1957 to join Art
Blakey's Jazz Messengers, he quickly instilled in New York-
based musicians an awesome respect for his talents.'

On April 6th 1957 Johnny made the celebrated Blue Note
album, *A Blowin' Session* with himself as leader and an all-star
band consisting of Lee Morgan, John Coltrane, Hank
Mobley, Wynton Kelly, Paul Chambers and Art Blakey.
Morgan and Kelly were at this time in the Dizzy Gillespie
Big Band, Mobley was with Horace Silver and Coltrane and
Chambers had been in the recently disbanded Miles Davis
Quintet. The story goes that Griffin, Morgan and the
rhythm section were outside the Birdland Club in
Manhattan waiting for a boat to take them across the
Hudson River to the Rudy Van Gelder studios in
Hackensack, New Jersey, when John Coltrane appeared.
Griffin and Alfred Lion of Blue Note asked Coltrane if he
would like to join in the session. This, as the album note says,
brought the tenor saxophone's two most technically auda-
cious stylists together for the only time on record.

In fact, Johnny Griffin outshines both Coltrane and
Mobley, not just in the matter of his awesome technical command and lightning technique, but also his ever-creative

improvisation. 'But,' says Johnny, 'the date wasn't competitive. Hank, Trane and I weren't trying to outblow each other. Of course, it might have been different if Sonny Stitt had been on the session!'

Griffin did six more recording sessions with Blakey between April and October 1957. The first of these, *Theory of Art* for the Bluebird label, recorded on April 2nd, teamed him with Bill Hardman and Lee Morgan (trumpet), Melba Liston (trombone), Sahib Shihab (alto saxophone), Cecil Payne (baritone saxophone), Wynton Kelly (piano) and Spanky De Brest (bass). The date produced just two tracks – 'A Night at Tony's' and 'Social Call'.

Theory of Art
RCA Victor
compilation CD

The second session took place six days later and resulted in the RCA album, *A Night in Tunisia*, featuring Bill Hardman, Jackie McLean (alto saxophone), Sam Dockery (piano) and Spanky De Brest. Recalling the date, Johnny says, 'One Sunday night at the Bohemia, we finished the gig at three in the morning and Blakey said to the guys, "Oh, I forgot to tell you – we have a record date tomorrow at one o'clock, so

make sure you get to the studio on time." I was staying at
Art's house at the time and the next day we arrived at the
studio two hours behind schedule. The a&r man was pulling
his hair out. No one had had any breakfast, so we all go out
for something to eat and we get back at four o'clock. Then
Blakey said, "OK, everybody stand in the corner and write a
tune." I wrote a piece called 'Off the Wall' and Jackie
McLean wrote something else. But, despite the rush and
panic, the date turned out very well.'

In his liner note for the album, Nat Hentoff said of Johnny
Griffin: 'Among the younger jazzmen tempered by the Blakey
heat in this set is the urgent Chicago tenor, Johnny Griffin,
whose arrival in New York ignited the interest and imagina-
tion of several established jazzmen.'

Says Griffin, 'It was fun, fun, fun all the time with Blakey,
and at that time the American jazz scene was really thriving.
Art could tour the whole country, playing mostly in clubs
from Washington to Wilmington, Philadelphia, Pittsburgh,
Detroit, Columbus, Cincinnati, Cleveland, Milwaukee, St.
Louis, Indianapolis, Chicago – right across the country –
Kansas City, Denver – then to San Francisco, Seattle,
Portland, Vancouver – then to LA.'

On May 13th Johnny recorded four tracks with Blakey for
the Jubilee label, together with Bill Hardman, Sam Dockery,
Spanky De Brest and Louis 'Sabu' Martinez on percussion,
under the title *Dawn on the Desert* and his fourth album for
Art, *Jazz Connection* – recorded on May 14th and 15th, 1957 for
the Atlantic label – was distinguished by having Griff's future
leader – Thelonious Monk – on piano, together with Bill
Hardman and Spanky De Brest.

Griffin's fifth record date with Blakey took place on July
29th 1957 when, with Sam Dockery replacing Monk on

piano, he recorded three tracks for the Calliope label, and, on October 9th and 11th that year, he recorded *Hard Drive* for Bethlehem, with Bill Hardman, Sam Dockery or Junior Mance on piano and Spanky De Brest.

Before joining Monk, Johnny returned to Chicago and worked with Gene Ammons and Lester Young through the winter. Then he toured as a single with pick-up groups all over the USA.

On October 23rd 1957, he recorded his third Blue Note album, *The Congregation*, with Sonny Clark on piano, Paul Chambers on bass and Kenny Dennis on drums. Sonny Clark, from Pittsburgh, had previously worked with the Lighthouse All Stars and with Buddy DeFranco. Paul Chambers, also from Pittsburgh, was best known for his work with Miles Davis. He was with Miles for eight years, making him Davis' longest-serving sideman. For Kenny Dennis, a twenty-seven-year-old from Philadelphia, this album was his recording début.

Four months after this session, Johnny Griffin began a long and productive association with Riverside Records. The label had been launched in 1954 by jazz enthusiasts Bill Grauer and Orrin Keepnews with the aim of reissuing classic jazz and blues recordings from the 1920s by King Oliver, Ma Rainey, Jelly Roll Morton and Blind Lemon Jefferson, among others. But it substantially broadened its repertoire range and went on to become one of the leading modern jazz labels. In 1958 Riverside planned a recording session to include Thelonious Monk and Johnny Griffin.

Back in 1955, Griffin had played a two-week engagement with Monk at the Bee Hive in Chicago. The club, located on East 55th Street and South Harper Avenue, had opened in 1948. Writing about the occasion in the liner note to Johnny's

Chicago Calling album, Joe Segal, owner of Chicago's famous
Jazz Showcase, observed: 'Johnny's two-week stay with Monk
at the Bee Hive in Chicago recently was one of the Hive's all-
time musical highlights in its ten-year history of presenting
jazz.'

Says Johnny, 'I will always remember the two weeks I
played with Monk at the Bee Hive. We had Wilbur Ware on
bass and Wilbur Campbell on drums. They were resident in
the Bee Hive. I was sitting at home, watching television, and
they called me and said they needed a saxophone player. I
didn't even know Monk was in town. I went over to the club
and joined the guys on the bandstand.

'I didn't know Monk's music. We had no rehearsal. He just
started playing and I had to figure out what he was doing.
But I'm never nervous or uptight about playing with people
because, for me, music transcends all personalities. So I only
listen to the music, not the personalities – so you can't over-
awe me with somebody no matter what their ability is
because, in the final analysis, there is only music and that has
always been my goal – to play music.'

When Monk returned to New York, he met Orrin
Keepnews, talked about the Bee Hive sessions and was full of
praise for Johnny Griffin. So much so that Keepnews decided to add Griffin to the Riverside roster. As he remembers:

'Monk was very excited about Johnny and bassist Wilbur
Ware. He said of Griffin, "He can play" – and, in Monk
speak, that meant that he was damn' good. As it turned out,
I was a little late because, even though I acted as promptly as
I could on Monk's recommendation, Johnny had already
been discovered and signed by Blue Note and had recorded
the *Introducing Johnny Griffin* album.'

Griffin made his début Riverside recording – *Johnny Griffin Sextet* – on February 25th 1958. This date was intended to be with Thelonious Monk, Sonny Rollins and Art Blakey, but the session didn't quite go according to plan.

'The original idea,' says Keepnews, 'was to have Monk on piano with Johnny, Donald Byrd, Sonny Rollins, Wilbur Ware and Art Blakey. But a certain amount of confusion ensued. I asked Monk to notify Art Blakey and Sonny Rollins about the date, but somehow or other he didn't make contact with the two guys so they never showed up in the studio. So we brought in Philly Joe Jones in place of Blakey and, in place of Rollins, Donald Byrd suggested Pepper Adams – so he came in.

'Well, we did one number, then Monk decided that things weren't working out the way he wanted, so he split. As I had a bunch of musicians in the studio and I was going to have to pay them anyhow, I consulted with Johnny and we went ahead, with Kenny Drew taking over from Monk.'

In his note for the album, Orrin Keepnews wrote, 'Griffin's two most notable qualities are his dexterity and his roots. "Roots" simply means that this is not one of those modernists who thinks that a reference to an old-time jazzman probably means Charlie Parker. Johnny has a deep awareness of who and what preceded him. He has been described as "influenced" by Sonny Rollins, but any similarities that may exist between these two talented contemporaries seem more a matter of a shared regard for the deep-toned tenor tradition of men like Coleman Hawkins, Ben Webster and Don Byas. Griffin includes these three on the roster of those who have affected his playing, along with Lester Young, Dexter Gordon and (inevitably) Bird . . . Perhaps even more importantly, there is in Griffin's warm, early music the rich influence of the blues and of the gospel-linked jazz often called "church blues".'

The day after the Sextet date, Griff made a quartet recording – *Way Out* – with the same rhythm section.

After these sessions, Griffin, who was staying at Art Blakey's apartment, got a call from Thelonious Monk: an invitation to join him at the Five Spot Café where Monk had been resident since June 1957. Johnny had also had an offer from Dizzy Gillespie, but he chose to go with Monk. 'I admired Monk's music and I couldn't let that opportunity pass. I accepted the offer without hesitation, because I loved Thelonious.'

Album sleeve: Thelonious Monk recorded at the Five Spot Café, New York City, August 1958, with Johnny Griffin, Ahmed Abdul-Malik and Roy Haynes, 2-LP set issued by Milestone Records 1977.

7

Looking at Monk

Who was this legendary figure whose quartet Griffin joined in the spring of 1958?

On March 6th 1965, I spent nine hours interviewing Thelonious Sphere Monk for the UK music weekly, *Melody Maker*. He was in Paris to appear at the Olympia Theatre with his quartet, which featured Charlie Rouse on tenor saxophone, Larry Gales on bass and Ben Riley on drums.

It was 7.30 pm and Monk had just finished a somewhat delayed breakfast in his thirty-dollars-a-day suite at the Prince de Galles Hotel. Big, bearded and benign, he came into the lounge with all the calm dignity of an illustrious potentate bearing gifts of cognac and Coke.

The impression was enhanced by a riotous, rainbow-striped dressing gown worn over slightly less bilious pyjamas. 'You must have a Hennessy,' he said gravely, and poured me enough brandy to fill a small goldfish bowl.

Monk didn't talk very much. If you get three words from him, I'd been told, you'll be doing very well. At least, I said to myself, that would be one more word than I got from Miles Davis when I approached him backstage at the Olympia, seeking an interview.

And, in fact, nine hours, one concert, five taxis and innumerable cognacs later, I'd completed the Monk interview.

'You've been described,' I began hopefully, 'as everything from a genius to a bluffer. How do you rate yourself?'

'I just try to play with feeling and beat. I play like myself – what I feel. I just happen to be a musician that people copy. When people say I'm controver-

Thelonious Monk

sial, I don't know what they mean. If they mean I don't play like anyone else, I guess that's right.'

'It's been suggested that your technique is limited.'

'What they mean – the people who say that – is that *their* technique is limited – because they can't do what I do. I'll tell you one thing – my playing seems to work. I get good audiences – people seem to enjoy it.

'I prefer concerts to club work – well, you get paid for one night at a concert as much as you do for a whole week in a club.'

At the age of forty-seven, Monk was at the peak of his career. His standing in the jazz world, after long, long years of unswerving dedication to his own musical principles, had never been higher and, for the previous two years, he had scarcely stopped working.

Yet there was a time when he was regarded as thoroughly

unreliable and unpredictable. It was said that he frequently failed to turn up for gigs, or arrived hours late.

'The record proves,' he said, 'that this is the biggest bunch of lies. I suppose people just like to run their mouth off. You know, some people were billing me for their concerts without asking me to play. My name would bring people in, then, when I didn't turn up, the promoters would say, "That's Monk."

'I don't know why people do these things. It's just lies. When I'm booked for a gig, I'm always there.'

I asked him why he never spoke to the audience at his concerts or told them which numbers he was playing.

'Well, I figure if they don't know what I'm playing, they'll find out if they're interested enough.'

Why did he always wear a hat on stage?

'People wear stage costumes. A hat is my stage uniform. Actually, it's not a hat – it's really a wig.'

Why did he sometimes use his whole forearm on the piano?

'That's the only way I can get that particular sound. It's not a gimmick – it produces a certain sound that I want at the time.'

Had he ever thought of switching to organ?

'No. I like piano. Organ is for funerals.'

What did he enjoy outside the realm of music?

'Ping pong,' he answered, without moving a muscle.

Of the dozens of original compositions he had contributed to jazz, which did he think was the best?

'''Round Midnight' is a pretty tune.'

At this point the conversation was interrupted by his Olympia concert. We resumed it some hours later when Monk, with his devoted wife, Nellie, was holding court in the

Left Bank jazz club run by Bud Powell's partner, Buttercup. Earlier, I had asked him to name some of his favourite musicians and had got nothing but an inscrutable smile.

I asked him again and he said, again smiling, 'You already asked me that. You trying to trip me up? I like any musicians who can play. If musicians can't play, I don't like them.'

'Do you think black musicians are generally better jazzmen than white musicians?'

He smiled again. 'I haven't heard them all. But I know some fine white musicians. I used some in my big band.'

Had he personally encountered any racial prejudice in the States?

'Not really. But then, I don't let things bug me. People let too many things bug them. I just don't worry. All worry gets you is more worry. I guess I'm a pretty happy cat. I got a wife and two kids and we all dig each other. I love music and I'm mentally rehearsing all the time. There is always something to learn in music, that's what makes it so interesting – if you're adventurous musically.

'What you said about technique – well, I can't play every idea that comes into my head immediately. But if it's hard to do, you got to practise until you can do it. You can always improve. I practise while I'm working, too. I've never really grieved about my technique.'

What did he think of the current jazz scene, with clubs struggling and a lot of good musicians out of work? 'If the clubs are closing, it's because they're charging too much for the whisky. And as for musicians out of work,' he said, looking me straight in the eye, 'well, I guess there are a lot of reporters out of work, too.'

As a postscript, I spoke to the person who probably knew Monk better than anyone – his wife, Nellie.

She told me that he was a homebody. Their two children, Thelonious Junior (fifteen) and Barbara (eleven), were both attending boarding school and Nellie always went on tour with Monk.

'But when he's not working, he loves to be at home. We play card games, talk, watch TV. And sometimes he'll sit all day at the piano, composing and practising. He's a very kind person, extremely honest and very good with the children. And musically, he's wonderful. I've heard people say he's a beginner – but Thelonious had as much formal musical training as anyone. I've heard him play faster than any other pianist – but he doesn't seem to want to do it now.'

Monk had an immense simplicity and a practically impervious serenity. He was not in the least hostile to interviewers – but simply uncommunicative and withdrawn. And, sometimes, you suspected that, if he didn't give much play to his tongue, it was because it spent a lot of time firmly lodged in his cheek.

Johnny Griffin joined him at the Five Spot Café early in 1958 and played six nights a week, together with Ahmed Abdul-Malik or Wilbur Ware on bass and Roy Haynes or Philly Joe Jones on drums. The club, located on Cooper Square, in New York's Bowery district, was owned by Joe and Iggy Termini. It had opened in the mid-1950s and specialized in presenting modern jazz groups. In 1956 it featured Phil Woods, with Duke Jordan, Art Taylor and Cecil Payne, and also Cecil Taylor.

'At our first rehearsal,' Johnny recalls, 'I asked Monk where the music was, and he said, "What music?" He had nothing written. He played a theme and once I'd got it together, I played it and he said, "OK, you got it." And that was it. Later, at the club, he got up during a number and went to the bar, leaving me alone for long, long minutes with the rhythm section.

'Monk and I hung out together. We were very close. He was quiet on and off the stand – but when he was hanging out with Art Blakey and me, he was different. He was the kind of person who wouldn't say a word for half an hour. The musicians would be running their mouths, babbling as was their wont, and Monk would say three words after half an hour and break everybody up – and that would destroy the whole conversation. He was really a humorist. He enjoyed his reputation of being enigmatic. Behind that façade of looking like Jomo Kenyatta and making people afraid to approach him, he was so human.'

Griffin told Digby Fairweather in a BBC Radio 2 interview in August 1991: 'Monk was one of the greatest musicians I've ever been around – if not *the* greatest. Monk and Art Blakey were great friends and when I was playing with Blakey, he was always trying to get Monk to come and play with him – which was ridiculous because Monk had Coltrane, Wilbur Ware and Shadow Wilson. And when I was working with Monk, he was trying to get Blakey to play with him in place of Roy Haynes. But after their gigs in New York, Monk and Blakey would hang out together and I'd be tagging along with them, either at my house or, more often, at Blakey's house.'

Leslie Gourse, in her biography of Monk, *Straight No Chaser*, records Johnny Griffin as saying that some people thought Monk was crazy, but, 'he was well aware of what was going on, very intelligent, learned and coherent when he wanted to do something. He had a way of putting people off, because he couldn't support idiots.

'Monk was an actor. He had no pretensions. He was natural, but he was always acting on stage. And he was always making gestures, getting up, dancing around in circles, patting his foot, stomping his heels. He was always like that. He didn't do anything without reason. He didn't play an extra note on the piano. He used space like a genius, and he taught a lot of musicians – Miles Davis and others – about space.'⁵

And in a December 2005 interview in Tel Aviv with journalist Ben Shalev, Griffin said, 'Monk didn't play bebop and he didn't play hard bop. He played Monk.'

The Termini brothers were afraid of Monk. After the first set at the Five Spot, when Monk showed no inclination to start the second, they would come to Griffin and beg him to persuade Monk to go on stage. There were always people lining up outside the café, waiting to get in, because Monk was such a great attraction. But he was always late. The first set was supposed to start at 9.30 pm, but it was generally at least one hour later before it got under way.

At this time, Johnny Griffin was playing Tuesday to Sunday with Monk at the Five Spot, and on Mondays at Birdland on Broadway, with Wynton Kelly, Paul Chambers or Wilbur Ware, and Philly Joe Jones.

The Five Spot engagement attracted a great deal of attention and certainly boosted Griffin's reputation. Many musicians visited the club, including Coleman Hawkins, Max Roach and Benny Goodman. Goodman invited Johnny to join his band, but Johnny was happy to stay with Thelonious.

On July 9th 1958, Monk's quartet made a live recording at the Five Spot, for the Milestone label, with Griffin, Abdul-Malik and Haynes. And on this occasion, Monk did manage to secure the services of Art Blakey. Art took over from Haynes on 'Bye Ya' and 'Epistrophy'.

Johnny Griffin went on to do one more Five Spot recording date with the quartet, on August 7th 1958 – a memorable session which included such classic Monk compositions as 'Rhythm-a-ning', 'In Walked Bud', 'Evidence', 'Blue Monk' and 'Misterioso'.

'Playing with Monk was always fun,' says Johnny. 'I admired him more than any other musician I've been around. He had a great personality and was one of the greatest comedians in the world. And he earned a place in the jazz hall of fame for his masterpiece, "Round Midnight', alone.

'Monk had a lot more technique than he normally cared to reveal. On one occasion, after a club gig, he told me that he could play like Art Tatum if he really wanted to. I said, "Get out of here, Thelonious – stop kidding me!" He replied, "Well, check this out." And he sat at the piano and executed a real Tatumesque run. I couldn't believe my ears or eyes. Then he said, "But I don't need that."'

The experience with Monk substantially broadened Griffin's harmonic and rhythmic conceptions. 'The way Monk composed was different and the way he related to rhythm was entirely different from anyone else I have ever played with,' says Johnny. 'It was very difficult to play his music with him comping on the piano at the same time. His comping was so strong. Intrusive. He could put his right hand down hard just when you least expected it. But if you listen to his records you'll find that, most of the time when I'm playing, he's not comping – I'd tell him, "Stroll." Monk was very agreeable – because we had a wonderful relationship. He would go to the bar and get us both a drink while I'd be playing with Roy Haynes and Ahmed Abdul-Malik.

'Playing his music, with him comping behind me, kind of put me in a straightjacket. Charlie Rouse did it fantastically, but for me it was like fighting – it was a war. I wanted to break through it, to do my thing.

'I wrote a tune as a tribute to Thelonious – 'A Monk's Dream' – which I first recorded on *The Return of the Griffin* album in October 1978. Ronnie Mathews was on that date – and he also loves Monk's music very much. He played some very Monkish things when I was soloing on that piece – and it had the same effect on me. I wanted to turn round and tell him to lay out. Now this is my own composition – but somehow, that Monkish accompaniment restricted me. Sometimes, people prefer to play without a piano in the group because the pianist has the whole orchestra at his fingertips and if he doesn't have that sympathy for what you are playing, he can get in the way. And that's what used to happen sometimes with Monk and me.'

* * *

But there was a far more serious problem that Griffin had to deal with at this point in his career. His alcohol consumption, already substantial when he was with the Lionel Hampton band, had increased alarmingly over the years, although he had developed a remarkable capacity to consume liquor without manifesting any apparent signs of inebriation – an attribute which could be regarded as a very mixed blessing.

Recalling his alcohol problems in a very frank interview with me in 1979, Johnny said:

'I woke up on New Year's Day in 1960 and I felt like somebody had struck me across my back with a baseball bat. I had terrible pains in my kidneys. So I went to Dr Schwarz on 116th Street [New York]. He told me that if you get to a reading of four for the liver, the liver has ceased to function. My reading was 3.78. He told me I was an alcoholic and said that I was on my way out – which I thought was very undignified. I contested his assertion and said he must be out of his mind, even though I had been out of my head for about twenty years.

'Anyway he told me I wasn't going to make it – and I said to myself, "I'll show you." So I stopped drinking for two weeks – and that was fantastic because I'd never stopped drinking in my life.

'I was very small as a child and when I was about eleven years old, my father used to give me beer, saying it was healthy because of the yeast content. But I didn't care much about the yeast content; it was the alcohol that was important. He'd give me a little beer for dinner. And when he wasn't looking, I'd go to where it was stashed and drink some more. During the war years, it was easy for a kid to get someone to get him a bottle of beer.

'When I joined Lionel Hampton in June 1945, I was drinking bad whiskey. But a dancer who was on the Hampton show told me not to drink that stuff and introduced me to Gordon's gin, not realising that my face was going to change into the face that was on the Gordon's gin bottle. I drank it straight, no chaser. I drank so much that I had to take vitamin B12 shots every week from a nurse. At seventeen, I was drinking a bottle a day, easily – and that went on until I was twenty. Then I went to see Dr. Schwarz.

'I drank continuously. It was amazing, because, when I arrived in New York all the big saxophone players – big guys like Ben Webster – called me junior. Though Ben would also call me some other names, like little bitty m.f. But I could go into the bar and drink those guys on to the floor, and I didn't weigh ninety pounds. I was less than five feet tall. I didn't pass the five-foot mark until I was twenty or twenty-one. Now I'm about five foot five and a half. By drinking alcohol, I was somehow able to make it. When I practised my instrument, I would be drinking while I practised. Because I thought, if I'm going to play this instrument in the club every night, I may as well have the same feeling all the time. Very logical.

'I drank with guys like Sonny Greer, Walter Page and Bud Freeman. Bud introduced me to the lady who was making corn whiskey across from the Apollo Theater in New York. I had all this help from saxophone players – they couldn't believe that I could drink so much alcohol and still be at least a little coherent, not falling over and able to make it on the tenor. I never had a problem getting around the instrument. I guess the drink must have had some effect on my reflexes – but I always felt good under the influence of alcohol and thought I was doing fine. People looked beautiful when I was high. I could stand them – but when I was sober, people didn't look so beautiful.

'Then, of course, there were the drugs. As a kid I smoked a little grass, but that was nothing. The heavier stuff, like cocaine and heroin, was introduced to me in 1948 when I was working with Joe Morris. I started to snort cocaine and horse for a couple of years. Then, one day in New York City, looking at myself in the mirror, I could see that I was deteriorating – I didn't look as clean as I should have been – so I left Joe Morris' band, went back to my mother's house in Chicago, put my horn in the corner and went and lay down in the grass in Washington Park. I just cleansed myself of everything, including alcohol. That was in the summer of 1950.

'From that point on I had the occasional smoke but no hard drugs, but I went back to drinking. Later on, I had a little cocaine from time to time. I was still under the impression that cocaine was not habit-forming. I used to mix cocaine and heroin – cocaine by itself was like nothing. But when I stopped using, I had withdrawal symptoms. I thought I was really ill, until somebody came and gave me a little cocaine. I said, "Wow! I feel like Popeye after eating spinach." And I hate spinach. I realized that I had been strung out. So I put those hard drugs behind me.'

* * *

Johnny left the Thelonious Monk group in the autumn of 1958 because he wasn't making enough money. He spent the next year travelling around the States and working with local rhythm sections, 'which,' he says, 'in many cases, were pretty inept. Well, it was the normal thing.'

He augmented his income by doing numerous record dates for Riverside, including the Philly Joe Jones album, *Blues For Dracula,* recorded on September 17th 1958, with Nat Adderley, Julian Priester, Tommy Flanagan and Jimmy Jones.

But despite a busy freelance schedule, it was still a struggle to make ends meet. He was living in a New York apartment and his wife was living in Chicago with their three children – boy and girl twins, John Arnold IV and Joanna, who had been born on March 14th 1955, and Ingrid, who had come into the world on November 1st 1958. Joan and Johnny found that the combination of this year-long separation and the increasing financial problems was putting a great strain on their relationship.

So, in 1961, Griffin's wife decided to move to New York in an effort to save the marriage. Says Joan, 'One day I sat down with Johnny in Chicago and pointed out that he had been home with us only thirty days out of the past year. So I left the children with Johnny's mother, moved into Johnny's apartment at 410 Central Park West and then, six months later, I went to Chicago and brought the children back to

New York. We all lived together for a while – but it just didn't work out. So, in 1962, Johnny moved into a hotel on Broadway, right across the street from Birdland.

'There were endless financial problems – and that's enough to destroy any marriage. But Johnny is one of the best people I've ever met. Most people marry for the things we broke up about! You know, when our kids see us together, talking and laughing and looking back on the past, it fills them with awe. And when I tell them how wonderful their father is, they look at me as if I'm crazy. "If he's so wonderful," they're saying to themselves, "why aren't you two together?"'

* * *

In September 1958, Griffin joined Nat Adderley to record the Riverside album, *Branching Out*, with Gene Harris (piano), Andy Simpkins (bass) and Bill Dowdy (drums), and then in July the following year he was back in his home city where he teamed up with trumpeter Ira Sullivan to record the album, *Blue Stroll*, for the Chicago label, Delmark. The rhythm section was one hundred per cent Chicagoan – with Jodie Christian on piano, Victor Sproles on bass and Wilbur Campbell on drums. In addition to tenor saxophone, Griffin also played alto and baritone and Sullivan doubled on baritone saxophone and peck horn.

Recalling the occasion in a June 1979 interview with Joe Goldberg on the New York radio station, WKCR-FM, he said, 'Oh my God! We recorded after the gig at six o'clock on a Sunday morning. We were all out of our minds. Completely shattered.' And, as Bob Koester observes in the note for the 1997 CD reissue of the album, not everything went according to plan. The band recorded in a tiny studio in Chicago's Old Town area run by the session musician, Richard Cunliffe.

Writes Koester, 'The bathroom doubled as echo-chamber. Wilbur had to borrow a very cheap set of drums when he discovered his own equipment had been locked in the ballroom of the Sutherland Hotel. The replacement served until a spur gave out part-way through 'Bluzinbee', which forced Wilbur to conclude the take with his bass drum, etc, pitched at a 45-degree angle. At one point in the remarkable track, Cunliffe was able to change over from one Magnecorder to another when the tape ran out.'

The *Little Giant* album, recorded 1959.

In August 1959, Johnny Griffin teamed up with trumpeter Blue Mitchell and trombonist Julian Priester to record the Riverside album *The Little Giant* with Wynton Kelly, Sam Jones and Al Heath.

The following year, he broke new ground with an album titled, *The Big Soul Band*. This presented a collection of gospel melodies, arranged by Norman Simmons and played by Clark Terry and Bob Bryant (trumpets), Matthew Gee and Julian Priester (trombones), Pat Patrick and Frank Strozier (alto saxophones), Griffin and Edwin Williams (tenor saxophones), Charles Davis (baritone saxophone), Harold Mabern and Bobby Timmons (pianos), Bob Cranshaw and Victor Sproles (basses) and Charlie Persip (drums).

The album, the product of recording sessions in New York on May 24th, May 31st and June 3rd 1960, was one of the first to feature jazz versions of gospel standards – such as 'Nobody Knows the Trouble I've Seen' and 'Deep River'. It was Johnny Griffin's salute to the founder of gospel music, the Chicago-based singer and songwriter, Thomas Dorsey, also known as Georgia Tom, whose songs combined religious texts with secular blues melodies. This connection with Johnny's home city was enhanced by the contributions of Chicagoans Bryant, Sproles, Priester and, above all, Simmons.

As producer Orrin Keepnews observes in the liner notes, the idea for the album was one which Griffin had had in mind for more than two years and the reason it took so long to come to fruition was that he had difficulty in finding an arranger whom he could trust to handle the project in the way he had in mind. It was when he recorded *The Little Giant*, nine months earlier, that the answer came to him.

As Keepnews relates, that album had featured 'three impressive, earthy tunes by the young Chicago pianist and arranger, Norman Simmons.' And when Johnny and Keepnews compared notes after that session, they were both certain that Simmons was the right man for the job.

Simmons at this time was on the road as accompanist to Dakota Staton, but, says Keepnews, 'he began working on the material in whatever time he could find in a half-dozen cities and, gradually, it all took firm shape.' Simmons wrote three compositions for the album, which also included Bobby Timmons' 'So Tired' and Junior Mance's 'Jubilation'.

In a note to the remastered version of the CD, released in 1990, Keepnews acknowledges that the band's execution of the scores, in some cases, is 'on the ragged side'. He adds, 'Since this was the very first time Riverside had been involved in anything as complex as eleven men and fully worked-out arrangements, and some of the musicians we had called were not all that experienced in that area, some of the ensemble passages are less than totally smooth . . . But it does provide a striking example of how strongly Johnny Griffin was playing and how imaginative were his improvisations over the full band background.'

Then, in September 1960, came *Studio Jazz Party*, a free-blowing jam session of a date with trumpeter Dave Burns, Norman Simmons, Victor Sproles and Ben Riley. It was followed, in February 1961, by *Change of Pace*, recorded with the unorthodox line-up of French horn (Julius Watkins), two basses (Bill Lee and Larry Gales) and drums (Ben Riley).

In July 1961, Griffin paid a moving and heartfelt tribute to Billie Holiday, with the album, *White Gardenia*, recorded with a large ensemble, which included Nat Adderley, Clark Terry, Ernie Royal, Jimmy Cleveland, Urbie Green, Barry Harris, Jimmy Jones, Barry Galbraith, Ron Carter, Ben Riley and a string section. The album featured ten Lady Day classics, including 'Good Morning Heartache', 'God Bless the Child', 'Don't Explain', 'Detour Ahead' and 'Travelin' Light'.

Griffin had a happy reunion with Thelonious Monk in the autumn of 1967 when George Wein set up a European tour for a Monk group that included Clark Terry, Ray Copeland, Jimmy Cleveland, Charlie Rouse, Phil Woods, Larry Gales and Ben Riley. The tour took in Rotterdam, Stockholm, Paris, Berlin and Mainz and for some of the dates, Johnny was added to the line-up. A number of recordings of the concerts were released by CBS, Unique Jazz, France's Concert and the Swedish Heartnote label.

8

Tough Tenors

The two-tenor partnership concept was memorably pioneered by Dexter Gordon and Wardell Gray in Hollywood on June 12th 1947, when they made their signal recording of *The Chase* for the Dial label, with pianist Jimmy Bunn, bassist Red Callender and drummer Chuck Thompson. The session was set up by Ross Russell, founder of Dial Records, and *The Chase* was released as a double-sided ten-inch 78 rpm record.

Over the next couple of decades, the tenors-in-tandem challenge was taken up by a number of top saxophonists – most notably, Al Cohn and Zoot Sims, Gene Ammons and Sonny Stitt, and Johnny Griffin and Eddie 'Lockjaw' Davis.

It was during an engagement at Birdland, in New York in 1960, that the Tough Tenors project was conceived. Since its star-studded opening on December 15th 1949, the venue had presented groups led by Charlie Parker, Lester Young, Stan Getz, Hot Lips Page and Max Kaminsky, and a new singing star, Harry Belafonte. Birdland, 'the jazz corner of the world', had become a hugely popular venue, committed principally to the bebop movement and presenting Dizzy Gillespie, Johnny Griffin, George Shearing, Maynard Ferguson, Thelonious Monk, Miles Davis, John Coltrane, Bud Powell and Erroll Garner. Located on Broadway, a few blocks west of 52nd Street, Birdland was run by Morris Levy, founder of Roulette Records, and managed by Oscar Goodstein. It closed in 1965 but was resurrected by John Valenti in 1986 at 2475 Broadway, on the corner of 105th Street. Then, in 1996, Birdland moved from the Upper West Side and returned to midtown Manhattan, at 315 West 44th Street.

'Birdland got to be my home,' says Griff. 'I played there opposite Charles Mingus, Horace Silver, Art Blakey, Maynard Ferguson and Quincy Jones, among others.' He also renewed his contact with Eddie 'Lockjaw' Davis, *aka* 'Jaws'. Born in New York on March 2nd 1922, Davis was a self-taught musician with a natural talent for jazz, and had played at Clark Monroe's Uptown House in late-1930s New York, less than a year after buying his first tenor saxophone.

Griffin had first met Davis when the Hampton band was playing a date in Philadelphia's Earl Theater. After the concert, he and Arnett Cobb went to the club where Jaws was then playing. Cobb and Jaws were vaguely related – Arnett had married one of Eddie's cousins. After that first meeting, Johnny joined Eddie for jam sessions on several occasions.

One night in Birdland in May 1960, during intermission, Griff was standing at the bar when Eddie Davis came into the club. Eddie had just disbanded the small group he had led since June 1956 with organist Shirley Scott, George Duvivier or Wendell Marshall on bass, and drummer Arthur Edgehill. As Griff and Jaws stood talking at the bar, they were joined by Babs Gonzales.

Says Griffin: 'Babs was stoned out of his mind that night in Birdland and he said, "Hey, you cats. Why don't you guys put it together? You don't want to go on working with those local rhythm sections."

'Babs knew I was unhappy with the pick-up bands I was using – the different rhythm sections. I was always crying because, while I got good musicians sometimes, there were other occasions when the rhythm section just wasn't up to scratch.'

Eddie Davis, who had had the idea of forming a two-tenor combo for some time, was due to follow Griffin into Birdland the following month, so Johnny and Jaws approached Oscar Goodstein and put the two-tenors project to him. Goodstein liked the idea and

Eddie 'Lockjaw' Davis

told them, 'OK, you finish this month out and then, next month, you can put the quintet together.' And that's how the Tough Tenors group came into being. It started with Chicagoans Norman Simmons on piano and Victor Sproles on bass – and Ben Riley, from Savannah, Georgia, on drums and the band cut its first album, *Battle Stations*, in September 1960 for the Prestige label.

For the next two albums, *Tough Tenors* and *Griff and Lock*, recorded for Jazzland on November 4th and 10th 1960, Junior Mance replaced Norman Simmons and Larry Gales took over from Victor Sproles. And on January 6th 1961, the

Tough Tenors quintet recorded eighteen titles for Prestige at the birthplace of bebop, the famous Minton's Playhouse in Harlem.

For their fifth record session, Eddie and Johnny decided to pay homage to Thelonious Monk by recording seven of his original compositions, including the virtually obligatory ''Round Midnight'. The album, *Looking at Monk*, was recorded on February 7th 1961 and, as sleeve note writer Chris Albertson noted, 'the idea for the album originally emerged from the fact that several Monk tunes had gradually become part of the quintet's working repertoire. In large part, this was due to the great fondness for this music felt by Griffin, who had been featured in Monk's quartet during most of 1958.' Albertson quoted Johnny as saying, 'There is a certain rhythmic freedom in almost all of his compositions that makes them ideal for us, since we always try to generate a feeling of freedom with this group.'

The Tough Tenors combo became a major attraction in clubs around Harlem. On one occasion, it was booked into Birdland for a week, playing opposite Stan Getz's quartet and Johnny and Eddie saw this as something of a challenge. Jaws said to Johnny, 'Listen, partner. I'm gonna tell you how we are going to get this guy. I'm gonna take him on the ballads and, on the fast numbers, you got him.'

Says Griffin, 'Boy, what a week that was! Every set was a battle.'

In his note for the *The Toughest Tenors* album, a compilation of tracks from five Jazzland albums which was released by Milestone 1976, Burt Korall wrote: 'Davis and Griffin competed but the music never took on the hostility of a cutting contest. It seemed a matter of mutual inspiration.' And Michael Cuscuna, in the liner for Dexter Gordon's 1978 CBS

Eddie 'Lockjaw' Davis and Johnny Griffin enjoying a joke.

album *Great Encounters*, notes that the quality of the tenor battles between Griff and Jaws 'drew as much from their dramatically contrasting styles as from their individual brilliance.'

Apart from his work with Davis, in the spring of 1962 Johnny Griffin took part in three star-studded Riverside recording sessions (February 27th, March 9th and April 16th), which provided the ten tracks for what proved to be Tadd Dameron's last album as leader – *The Magic Touch*. Also participating were trumpeters Joe Wilder, Clark Terry, Ernie Royal and Charlie Shavers; French horn player Julius Watkins; trombonists Jimmy Cleveland and Britt Woodman; Leo Wright and Jerry Dodgion on alto sax and flute; Jerome Richardson on tenor sax and flute; baritone saxophonist Tate Houston; pianist Bill Evans; bassists George Duvivier and Ron Carter; drummer Philly Joe Jones and vocalist Barbara Winfield.

Dameron, who has been hailed as 'the definitive composer/arranger of the bebop era', wrote such memorable bop standards as 'Good Bait', 'The Squirrel', 'Hot House', 'Our Delight', 'Lady Bird', 'Dameronia', as well as 'Look, Stop and Listen' and 'If You Could See Me Now' – both of which are featured on *The Magic Touch*.

In New York, on May 3rd 1962, Griff and Jaws recorded some further tracks for Prestige, with Horace Parlan on piano and celeste, Buddy Catlett on bass and Arthur Taylor on drums, on which they departed from the tandem tenor idea and did individual quartet tracks. None of the twelve numbers features the two together. Also, the recording consists principally of ballads – except for the mid-tempo title waltz, 'Pisces', a Griffin original. For some inexplicable reason, it took the better part of forty years for the album to be released.

'The Tough Tenors combo broke up in 1962,' says Johnny, 'because we were paying the rhythm section more money than we were making. We always had good crowds but we never had any money.'

The last Tough Tenors album, *Tough Tenor Favourites*, was recorded on February 5th 1962, with Horace Parlan, Buddy Catlett and Ben Riley.

In his note to the Tough Tenors' 1961 album, *Live at Minton's*, Crispin Cioe notes that the quintet broke up in 1962 'out of necessity' and he quotes Jaws as saying:

'We couldn't keep the group going after two years because we started losing money on it. Club owners felt it was just too much saxophone. And clubs were in a slump too. The avant-garde, 'free' thing was coming in, which journalists pushed, so that a lot of young players started going in that direction.'

Says Orrin Keepnews: 'This was a reasonably successful group, they recorded, they worked, but I think Johnny saw it

Pisces album sleeve (Original Jazz Classics): Eddie 'Lockjaw' Davis (*left*) and Griffin, recorded May 1962.

as a kind of dead end – he was also having some unhappiness in his personal life.'

The Tough Tenors concept would be revived in April 1970 when Davis and Griffin recorded the album, *Tough Tenors Again 'n' Again*, for the German MPS label, with Francy Boland (piano), Jimmy Woode (bass) and Kenny Clarke (drums). Griffin and Davis teamed up for further Tough Tenors dates in 1977 and 1984.

Recalling his partnership with Jaws, Johnny said: 'After I'd finished playing, I would maybe go to the bar and get a drink or sit down on the floor in front of the drums. Jaws was standing there like a soldier at attention. I asked myself, "What kind of partner have I got here?"

'One night in Birdland, peering through the haze of the alcohol that I had drunk, I looked at Jaws and he looked back at me exactly like Huckleberry Hounddog[6] – and it burst out of my mouth. That's what I called him!

'Immediately I said to myself, "Oh my God, what have I done?" I thought he was going to kill me – but then his sense of humour prevailed and he started to laugh. Eddie had a keen sense of humour. He once told Arthur Taylor that the only reason he played tenor was because saxophone players got all the nice girls. He said, "By the time you got the drums packed up, Arthur, the horn players have gone off with the best chicks."

'Eddie's principal influence was Ben Webster – in fact, Ben would call him "Little Ben". But no one could play like Jaws – it seemed to me that he was actually chewing the mouthpiece up when he played. He insisted on rehearsing seven tunes at a time. We'd rehearse the seven tunes, then the next day we would get the rhythm section together and go through the tunes with them. In the end we must have had about eighty tunes in our heads which we could play at any time.'

Johnny and Eddie became lifelong friends. Davis said he enjoyed working with a saxophonist like Griffin who could really play 'because we inspire each other. Everyone has off-nights and so the one who's feeling better helps the other one. We are trying to bring back older tunes with a different flavour – tunes with more substance and feeling to them – that get in that good groove. Many composers today tend to get too cold and mathematical. We don't want that "space music"; we don't want to get too far away from the public.'

Despite the difference in character, there was a remarkable musical rapport and compatibility between Griff and
Jaws. Joe Goldberg described Jaws as 'a shrewd and mordant
observer of almost anything you care to name and something
of a home made philosopher who will draw upon a vast range
of interests, with vocabulary to match.'

Says Johnny Griffin: 'At first the relationship was a little
difficult – we had completely different personalities – I was
wild, Jaws was conservative.

'Eddie was punctilious about time and not being late for
the gig, but I was a little bit more laid-back and casual – so
sometimes I was somewhat less than punctual. I'd leave
everything until the last minute.' So Eddie presented Johnny
with an alarm watch, engraved 'To Griff from Jaws', which
Johnny still treasures: 'He would set the alarm for forty-five
minutes before we hit, which should have given me enough
time to get across town and onto the stand. But I was usually late.

'Jaws liked to go to after-hours joints, sit at the bar and
expound on his knowledge of worldly events. One night in
East St Louis when we finished working, he was making out
the payroll and he asked me a question – something about
African politics. I answered the question and when he realized that I knew a little bit about world affairs, he looked at
me in a different light. He got to be like my brother. I miss
him sorely.'

As Bob Houston observed in his note for the MPS album
Tough Tenors Again 'n' Again, 'Like many a good group and true
before them, their robust quintet fell foul of the over-com-
petitive world in which the ability to make good jazz rarely
coincides with making a good living.'

In June 1963 Davis decided to give up full-time playing and

Griff and Jaws in 1961 (photo Esmond Edwards).

work as a booking agent. Commenting very pertinently on the US jazz scene to Stanley Dance in a *Down Beat* interview in November 1964, he said:

'According to the older hands, they've never seen it this bad . . . Jazzwise, there's a combination of reasons. A lot of the club owners have found very few winners. The conduct of many jazz artists hasn't helped – the same old problems of showing up late but a little more profound. Jazz at one time was a happy thing, but now it has become so serious, even depressing in some instances. And there are too many experiments going on now. The experiments should be in the studio, because you cannot expect an audience of musicians every night.

'Club owners claim there's a lack of entertainment on and off the bandstand. The relationship with the patrons is so distant. The artists stay in the bandroom during intermission or leave the premises and the patrons feel this. The effect of a small group in a nightclub was to bring the artist and the patron close, in a way big bands on stage never could. The patrons enjoyed this, and it was a success. Today a lot of them say they are afraid to go and ask the name of an artist's latest record.

'The need for entertainment can mean that music will go in one of two directions. Maybe the older musicians and their values will be accepted again, or maybe the younger musicians will be groomed to realize the need for entertainment. Either way, it doesn't mean you have to become a clown.'

Recalling his Tough Tenors days, Eddie Davis told Dance, 'There were Gene Ammons and Sonny Stitt, Wardell Gray and Dexter Gordon, but I don't believe any two-tenor unit stayed together so long and travelled the country as much as Johnny Griffin and I did.'

Eddie Davis rejoined the Basie band as a major soloist and road manager in 1965 and stayed with the Count until 1973, after which he worked principally with Ella Fitzgerald and Harry Edison.

Record producer Gigi Campi was a Tough Tenors enthusiast and when Davis joined the Kenny Clarke–Francy Boland Big Band to record the *Sax No End* album for SABA (later MPS) on June 18th, 1967, Campi resolved that, when the opportunity arose, he would record Jaws and Griff with the band's rhythm section of Francy Boland, Jimmy Woode and Kenny Clarke. He achieved this aim in 1970 with the *Tough Tenors Agan 'n' Again* album for MPS.

9

Wailing with Wes

On June 25th 1962, Johnny Griffin recorded a veritable landmark album for the Riverside label when he joined guitar virtuoso Wes Montgomery and the rhythm section of Miles Davis' sextet for a live concert. The resulting LP, *Full House*, is widely considered to have been one of the most outstanding of the forty-plus albums recorded by Montgomery in the course of his twenty-year professional career. And it certainly ranks among the very best in Griffin's prolific and diverse discography.

The album was recorded in the Tsubo coffee house, located on Telegraph Avenue in Berkeley, California, in a building which also housed the Berkeley jazz station, KJAZ-FM.

John Leslie 'Wes' Montgomery was born on March 6th 1925 in Indianapolis, Indiana. His elder brother, Monk, was a bassist and his younger brother, Buddy, played vibraphone and piano. Wes began learning guitar when he was twelve, playing on a four-string tenor instrument which his brother, Monk, had bought for him.

'He had no formal musical training,' remembers Johnny, 'but he had a fantastic natural aptitude. And he was great to work with. He had an unassuming nature, was always calm and composed and was a truly phenomenal musician.'

What distinguished Montgomery from his fellow jazz guitarists was his remarkable use of octaves and block chords, as well as the great fluency of his single-line playing – plus the fact that he used his thumb instead of a plectrum. In 1943, when he was nineteen, he heard Charlie Christian's recording of *Solo Flight* and was hugely impressed. So much so that, the next day, he went out and bought an electric guitar and

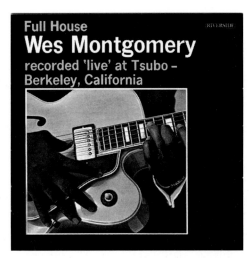

Full House   RIVERSIDE

Wes Montgomery

recorded 'live' at Tsubo –
Berkeley, California

CD insert for
Full House,
recorded
1962.

amplifier for $350, money which he could ill afford. He then proceeded to learn, note for note, all the Charlie Christian solos that he heard on records.

Montgomery had joined Lionel Hampton's band in 1948, just a year after Johnny Griffin's departure. After leaving Hampton in January 1950, he began leading his own small groups and was signed up by Riverside in 1959, remaining with the label until 1963. Between April 1958, when he recorded the album *Montgomery Land* for Pacific Jazz with his two brothers plus tenor saxophonist Harold Land and drummer Tony Bazley, and May 1968, Wes made more than forty albums, featuring among others: Johnny Griffin, Cannonball Adderley, Freddie Hubbard, Jimmy Smith, Tommy Flanagan, Victor Feldman, Hank Jones, Melvin Rhyne, Clark Terry, Harold Mabern and Ronnie Scott.

His second album for Riverside, *The Incredible Jazz Guitar of Wes Montgomery*, earned him *Down Beat* magazine's New Star award in 1960. He went on to win the *Down Beat* Critics' Polls as top jazz guitarist in 1960, 1961, 1962 and 1963. One of the most influential and innovative jazz guitarists, Wes Montgomery died of a heart attack on June 15th 1968. In a tribute to him, Joe Pass said, 'To me, there have only been three real innovators on the guitar – Wes, Charlie Christian and Django Reinhardt.'

The *Full House* session was a dream come true for producer Orrin Keepnews, as he graphically recorded in the notes he wrote for the album:

'Ever since the first time I heard Wes Montgomery – which was on the stand in a club – I have been among those anxious to have a live record come into being. But not just any old "live" date would do. All concerned wanted to wait for the best possible set-up: the right time, the right place, the right supporting cast.

'Then, early in June of 1962, Wes telephoned from California with news that all the necessary ingredients seemed to be at hand. He was in San Francisco. The Miles Davis Sextet was in town – meaning that the magnificent and close-knit rhythm unit of Wynton Kelly, Paul Chambers and Jimmy Cobb was available. Also in the city was tenorman Johnny Griffin. All these were men between whom there was considerable mutual respect. Furthermore, Wes had some new tunes that he felt would go very well in quintet form. Just across the bay, in the city of Berkeley, was a coffee house exotically named "Tsubo"; Wes had worked there with his brothers and was excited about the far better than average acoustics of the place. Last, but surely not least, the jazz audiences of that area are wonderfully stimulating people to play for.

'It was decided to record in Tsubo on a Monday, when his chosen associates would be having a night off from their regular jobs; and Wes began at once to make the group familiar with the material. On June 25th, as engineer Wally Heider began to set up his equipment, it became obvious that the only audience problem might be one of excess – alerted by local newspaper stories and word-of-mouth, the faithful were arriving early, and long before starting time the modest-sized club was packed to the doors. Actually, the line outside the door stretched around the corner all night long, and there was also a permanent outdoor audience in a parking lot next-door, listening via the loudspeakers in the "control room" we had set up in a storeroom behind the club! In short, the title *Full House* (which originally struck me as a suitable reference to a group of five consisting strictly of kings and aces) can be taken as an entirely factual description of the setting for this album.

'I propose to let the music contained herein speak for itself. Most of the tracks are on the long side, deliberately, for one major reason. For recording Wes "live" was to capture the breathtaking way he can *build* a solo through chorus after chorus. Too often the term "stretching out" really means nothing more than a lengthy and eventually tiresome solo stint; but the manner in which Wes constructs his solos is something else, bringing into play his amazing sense of dynamics and his "impossible" octave and block-chord effects. Even such always-fiery and tasteful soloists as Griffin and Kelly seem to have picked up an extra spark or two from Wes on this occasion.

'So, without in any way detracting from the vigour and importance of past and future Wes Montgomery records, it can certainly be said that this album, capturing a brilliant jazz artist under the best of circumstances, is something truly special.'

Not only is the music on this album and the compatibility of the musicians of the highest order, but the sound quality is also remarkably good.

On the following day, Johnny was back in the Tsubo coffee house to record the album, *Do Nothin' till You Hear from Me*, with Buddy and Monk Montgomery and Arthur Taylor. This time the session took place after the club had closed for the night.

A little less than three years later, on March 27th 1965, Griffin, then resident in Paris, had the opportunity to work once again with Wes Montgomery in a live concert at the Théâtre des Champs-Elysées. Happily, the performance was recorded by the independent French label, BYG, and, once again, a superb album – *Wes Montgomery Live in Paris* – resulted.

It was Alan Bates who brought Wes to Europe and organized the Paris concert. Wes had arrived two days earlier to appear with his quartet in the BBC's *Jazz 625* television programme. With him were Harold Mabern on piano, Arthur Harper on bass and Jimmy Lovelace on drums. The quartet is featured on seven of the tracks of the album and, for the final three, Johnny Griffin joins the group.

When you listen to the astonishing technical facility demonstrated by Griffin in his thirty-eight whirlwind choruses on 'Blue and Boogie', you have to acknowledge that comparing his technique to that of Tatum is not an entirely fanciful analogy.

I was fortunate enough to be covering the concert for *Melody Maker* and I wrote the following review:

'Billed as the greatest guitarist in jazz, Wes Montgomery made his first appearance in Paris on Saturday at the Théâtre des Champs-Elysées and scored a resounding success . . . Montgomery gave a memorable display of virtuoso guitar playing – rich chord work, incredibly sweet single-note runs and those famous octave and double-octave effects.

'And, on top of his unparalleled technique, Montgomery demonstrated his almost unlimited powers of invention and a superb ability to swing. He played with great assurance and had a real feeling for the music. But what really brought the concert to exciting life was the appearance of Johnny Griffin, who played a few numbers with the rhythm section and then was joined by Montgomery who closed the performance.

'Griffin played magnificently and was especially inspired on a breakneck version of 'Indiana', switching alternate choruses between A flat and F. His 'Body and Soul' was a masterpiece and on 'Blue Monk' he knocked everyone out when the rhythm section laid out and he played a breathtaking series of unaccompanied choruses.

'Montgomery, clearly inspired by Griffin, was at his supreme best when the two men were back together on stage. He impressed as an immensely happy jazzman who listens appreciatively and attentively to what his fellow musicians are doing.

'It was the most swinging concert Paris has seen in a long time.'

Six days after that concert, Wes played a date in Amsterdam with Clark Terry and then a week at Ronnie Scott's Club with Stan Tracey, Rick Laird and Ronnie Stephenson. Ronnie Scott and Johnny Griffin were back with Wes again for a date in Hamburg on April 30th, when they recorded *Live in Europe* for Philology, with Hans Koller, Ronnie Ross, Martial Solal, Michel Gaudry and Ronnie Stephenson.

10

First Taste of Europe

In the early 1960s, Johnny Griffin found that engagements in the United States were becoming increasingly hard to come by. He remembers:

'I had lunch one day with Riverside's Bill Grauer at the Paramount Hotel, where the record company had its offices, and he said to me, "Johnny, I've been watching you and I think, if you go to Europe, you probably won't come back." I couldn't imagine what he meant by that, because I felt I was in New York City and that was heaven already. Where could I go after heaven?'

Bill Grauer had fallen in love with Europe and spent as much time on that continent as he possibly could. Orrin Keepnews believes it was Grauer, more than anyone else, who convinced Johnny that he should head for Europe, where he would find recognition, respect, and a level of work that he would not necessarily find in the States. Johnny also recollects that 'Grauer got me to promise that I would go on the next European promotional tour for Riverside in December 1962.'

The tour, taking in Paris, Brussels, Stockholm, London and several locations in Holland, was set up by Alan Bates, a

Paris-based jazz enthusiast who was running the Interdisc distribution company which represented Riverside, among other labels. Says Bates, 'We decided that, in order to build up sales, we needed to bring some of the artists to Europe on promotional tours – and one reason why I wanted to have Johnny Griffin on tour, apart from the fact that he was a superb musician, was that I was a frustrated, would-be tenor saxophone player.'

Griffin arrived in Paris in December 1962. He was scheduled to play a one-month engagement at the Blue Note, starting on December 12th, with Kenny Drew, French bassists Gilbert Rovere or Michel Gaudry and Larry Ritchie or Charles Bellonzi on drums. In the Blue Note, he had the pleasant surprise of meeting up with his old friend, Bud Powell. 'I didn't know he was in Paris,' says Johnny, 'but it was a great pleasure to see him again and to play with him once more. The last time I had seen Bud was in 1958 or 1959, when I was working in the Village Vanguard with Cedar Walton. Bud came into the club and, when we finished the set, he went on to the stand and started playing. He just wouldn't stop and he was burning! We finally had to drag him off the piano.'

After making his first European tour in 1956 with the Birdland All Stars, Bud Powell had settled in Paris in 1959 and worked regularly at the Blue Note with Pierre Michelot and Kenny Clarke over the next three years.

Griffin's first impressions of Europe, and of Paris in particular, were extremely positive: 'In Europe, I really learned how to relax. I never knew how to relax in America. I was on a treadmill in New York, running all the time and going no place. I went from Beefsteak Charlie's to record company to booking agency and then back to Beefsteak Charlie's every day. A complete dead-end – and everything was a rush. If I go down the street, I'm running – never taking my time.

'But the French had this *doucement* attitude. At first it exasperated me. But then I saw how much the people were enjoying life. There was a moment in Paris which really made me think about that American lifestyle. I was staying in this hotel and I picked up the phone at around 11.30 one morning and asked for a number. The guy on the desk told me the line was busy and he said he'd try again in a few minutes. I waited half-an-hour. Then I picked up the phone again and tried to reach the reception desk. No answer. So I go downstairs to the reception desk – and the guy's gone to lunch. When he finally came back, I told him I'd been waiting to get this call. He said to me, "Monsieur, vous êtes pressé!" And I thought to myself – he's right! What's the big rush? A matter of life and death? I'm going crazy about making a

Bud Powell (left) in Paris with Mike Hennessey, July 1961.

telephone call. So I said to myself, "Wait a minute, take your time, have a nice glass of Bordeaux and relax." The gracious way of living!

'The Europeans accepted jazz as American classical music. And they knew where you were born, your career background.'

In a radio discussion about the Little Giant, chaired by Nancy Wilson, Kenny Washington, a regular Griffin sideman from the late 1970s, said, 'The Europeans really took to Griff when he first arrived there. He finally began to get the respect he had so long deserved. He was able to jump right into that scene and start to make some respectable money. He can demand a price – and he gets it. He couldn't always do that in the States, because the people in the business here are too busy nickel-and-diming. And Johnny really doesn't have any time for that – and neither should he have.'[7]

Kenny Washington also paid tribute to the high degree of patience and tolerance Griffin evinced when dealing with the vagaries of truculent club owners, agents and promoters in the States.

'His ability to avoid conflict could sometimes be maddening – and I used to get into arguments with him about that sometimes. That was the only time we would fall out. I just felt he was so nice to these people, whereas I just wanted to take something and throw it at them – because they were totally disrespectful to us. But Griff would always find some middle ground and he would never get angry at those people – when he really needed to. But he always worked it out.'

Kenny admits that Johnny's consistent good nature and generosity have also been an inspiration. 'He's a very fair man – it's like he never really thinks about himself. For the most part he thinks about the cats – he's just a very good person to work with.'

As Orrin Keepnews has observed, 'Johnny Griffin is really a very nice guy – an admirable human being. In the period that I knew him best and worked with him most closely, he had a tremendous sense of loyalty. He had a regular recording contract with a company that used his work frequently and he made a point of hiring old friends and associates when he recorded – including a lot of Chicago musicians who were in New York, not necessarily working that much, but good players nevertheless. He is a man who has always looked after his friends.'

And one of Griffin's Chicago friends, guitarist George Freeman, fully endorses those sentiments: 'He is someone you can always count on. Johnny is like family to me.'

Kenny Clarke had been resident at the Paris Blue Note from January 1st 1959 but, towards the end of 1962, when he was working in the club with organist Lou Bennett and guitarist Jimmy Gourley, he was involved in a bitter argument with the owner of the club, Etla Benjamin – the Polish-born wife of its manager, Ben Benjamin, and a woman who, according to Jimmy Gourley, was totally obnoxious. The result of the dispute was that Clarke was fired.

The arrival in Paris of Johnny Griffin, the little giant from Chicago, who'd been making a name for himself in New York – notably at Birdland – in that Tough Tenors partnership with Eddie Lockjaw Davis, represented a very welcome development for Ben Benjamin, following the departure of Kenny Clarke.

Johnny had never met Clarke, but 'before I left New York, I ran into Max Roach, who lived just around the corner from my apartment building at 101, Central Park West. When I told him I was heading for Paris, he said to me, "When you see Klook, tell him the guys here are still trying to play what he laid down years ago." Some days later I met Kenny for the very first time. Our paths had never crossed in the States, but I'd seen him playing with Dizzy's band in the 1940s. Klook was now working at the Club St. Germain on the Left Bank. He met me outside the Blue Note – he wouldn't come in because of his falling-out with the management. But I gave him Max's message and I could see that it meant a lot to him.'

The number of self-exiled American jazz and blues artists in Paris at this time was quite substantial. In addition to Klook, Jimmy Gourley, Larry Ritchie and Kenny Drew, the musicians and singers included Chet Baker, Aaron Bridgers, Donald Byrd, Sonny Criss, Nathan Davis, Nancy Holloway, Mezz Mezzrow, Albert Nicholas, Bobbie Parker, Bud Powell, Hazel Scott, Art Simmons, Memphis Slim, Joe Turner and Benny Waters, among many others.

After the Blue Note engagement, Johnny left Paris to play dates in Sweden, Belgium and the UK and Nathan Davis took his place at the Blue Note.

In January 1963, Griff worked at the Golden Circle in Stockholm, where Jimmy Woode was the resident bassist. Then, in February, he played a benefit concert in Brussels for the Belgian saxophonist/clarinettist/flautist,

Don Byas – one of Johnny Griffin's great saxophone heroes.

Bobby Jaspar. There followed a four-week engagement at Ronnie Scott's Club in London's Gerrard Street with Stan Tracey (piano), Malcolm Cecil (bass) and Jackie Dougan (drums). At the end of February, he embarked on a two-week tour of Holland, with Pim Jacobs (piano), Ruud Jacobs (bass), Wim Overgaauw (guitar), Han Bennink (drums) and singer Rita Reys.

While he was in Holland, Johnny visited one of his great saxophone heroes, Don Byas, at his home. 'I had met him earlier,' says Johnny, 'when he came to the Sheherazade Club in Amsterdam where I was playing. It was *the* jazz club in Amsterdam and I had arrived early for a rehearsal. There were some press people there. I went straight to the bar and the press guys started interviewing me. But they didn't even know Don Byas – I couldn't believe it. I was very happy to discover that Don was living a healthy life. He wasn't drinking. He was scuba diving and riding around on a motor cycle. He was also teaching Dutch kids weightlifting. He was so surprised to see me and he said, "You haven't forgotten me?" And I said, "You kidding? No Don Byas, no Johnny Griffin." And that was the truth.'

Johnny Griffin returned to the United States in March 1963 – but not for long. In his interview with Arthur Taylor for *Notes And Tones*, Griffin says, 'I went from London back to New York and as soon as I got off the plane I felt like I was doomed. I said, "What am I doing back here?"'

11

Europe for Good

In May 1963, Griffin and his wife, Joan, decided to part for good. Their three children – boy and girl twins, John Arnold IV and Joanna, aged eight, and five-year-old Ingrid – went back to live with Johnny's mother in Chicago.

Says Johnny, 'We had been married for nine years, but our relationship had completely broken down. Everything was falling apart for me at that time. In addition to family troubles, I had financial problems and the jazz scene was really in decline. And when my music began to get sad, I asked myself, "Why stay and suffer? Goodbye New York!"

'I was in total disagreement with the major disc jockeys and so-called jazz critics of the day, who were proclaiming a new noise which they called music and which turned out to be avant-garde and free jazz and I thought it was all rubbish – which it proved to be.

'I'd come back to the States in March 1963, but in May I decided to go back to Europe for good. Bill Grauer was right about my not wanting to return to the USA after spending time in Europe. In addition, the Internal Revenue had decided that I owed them around $15,000 in back taxes. I tried to explain to them that it was impossible for me to owe them this amount of cash since I didn't have any money. They told me that didn't matter – I had had it! I told them that I was not a good record keeper and I couldn't understand where the money had gone. I was living a pleasurable life. Even when in trouble, have fun, that's my motto. But money and me have never been very good friends.

'When the crunch came, I was working at Birdland with my own group.

'The Birdland Corporation had been very nice to me. Oscar Goodstein, the manager of the club, hired me to play there four months out of the year – one month in every season – and that was a good base to work from. When I came off the stand one night, Oscar informed me that the Internal Revenue had been there to tell him that whatever money was due to me he had to give to them. They told the Riverside company the same thing. So I decided then and there that I was not going to support these people because I had been done a grave injustice. The IRS takes advantage of the little people and lets the big people go free.

'My friend, Babs Gonzales, came up with an idea to raise some money from Alfred Lion of Blue Note Records. It was Babs who had recommended me and Jimmy Smith to Alfred Lion and his partner, Francis Woolf, and he decided that he should get some commission for these valuable introductions. But when he went to the Blue Note offices, they wouldn't let him in. So he called them on the phone and made some kind of threat to them – he was that kind of character. In the end, Blue Note came up with about $3,000 – part cheque and part cash.

'While this was going on, I was waiting for Babs in Beefsteak Charlie's, the favourite watering hole for New

York musicians, right across the street from the old Greyhound bus station. Babs came back with the money – enough to buy some drinks and then to invest in two boat tickets on the *Rotterdam* to go to Europe.

'Babs and I caught the boat for Rotterdam in May 1963. We arrived in Amsterdam on May 19th and we played some gigs in Holland, which had been set up for us with the Jacobs brothers – Pim, the pianist, and Ruud the bass player. Babs and I rented a little house and stayed in Holland for a few weeks. Then Ben Benjamin invited me back to the [Paris] Blue Note. So I went back to Paris, where I was to live for the next ten years, and Babs returned to the States.

'Playing at the Blue Note was one of the main reasons for my going to Europe. Kenny Drew and Bud Powell were there. I worked in the club with Bud Powell, Kenny Drew, Lou Bennett, Bibi Rovere, Larry Ritchie, Kenny Clarke, Nathan Davis, Dexter Gordon and also with Art Taylor, who came to Paris in the summer of 1963. I would be booked into the Blue Note for four or five months at a time.'

Nathan Davis spent a lot of time with Johnny Griffin during this period. He remembers, 'We would practise together and I recall him telling me, "Nathan, one thing to remember – always play the blues, no matter what piece you're playing." And he meant "play with feeling" – which he always did.

'I will never forget that Johnny gave me one of my big breaks. Ray Charles had come to Paris to play a concert at the Salle Pleyel – this was some time in the mid-1960s. Ray's chief saxophone soloist, David 'Fathead' Newman, had missed the flight and Ray asked if Johnny could sub for him. Johnny said he wasn't able to do the gig and recommended me. The result was that I played the Salle Pleyel date and three other concerts with the Ray Charles orchestra.

'And what was so great about Griff was that he told Ray that he had to pay me the same fee that he had asked for. That was a really big opportunity for me.'

In Paris, Griffin stayed successively in the Louisiane, Napoléon and Rotary hotels and then took an apartment in the Nation district. Later he lived in a third-floor apartment in Pigalle, close to the home of Francis Paudras, where Bud Powell was living.

'At one period,' says Johnny, 'I was there in the Blue Note with Bud every night. Bud had a drink problem at this time. His problem was that he couldn't get enough of it. The Blue Note staff were under orders from Ben Benjamin to refuse him alcoholic drinks, but he would always try to outwit the staff by asking total strangers to buy the drinks for him.

'I'll never forget that scene in the *'Round Midnight* movie, when Dexter is standing at the bar of the Blue Note. Suddenly the man next to him falls backwards on to the floor. And Dexter says to the barman, "I'll have what he had." That was Bud! I saw that happen one night during intermission. Jacques, the barman, was instructed not to serve Bud anything stronger than some watered-down wine. Then this guy standing next to Bud collapses – and Bud says to Jacques, "Give me what he had."

'But then Bud got sick. He was staying in the Hotel Louisiane with his lady, Buttercup, and Francis Paudras, a devoted friend and admirer, was worried about him. He wanted Bud to come and stay in his apartment, where he could look after him. But Buttercup wouldn't let him have Bud. A tug of war developed between Paudras and Buttercup, so I went to the Louisiane, picked up Bud and brought him to Francis' house.

'He was coughing so badly that Francis took him to a hospital where a doctor friend of his examined Bud. It turned out that he had such contaminatory tuberculosis that he could have infected everybody around him. We all had to have X-rays. Buttercup didn't believe Bud was sick – she told me that the scars which showed up in the X-ray were old scars. But the doctor told Bud that if he had waited two more weeks in that hotel room, he would have been dead.

'I was living next door to Francis and I would see Bud almost every day. Sometimes he would go missing. On one occasion, a woman called to say she'd seen him in a café and we had to go and get him. They would put it out on the radio that he had gone missing.

'He got so fat while he was in hospital. He'd drink all the beer he could get and eat all the candies – like a little kid. But once he got back to the piano, he played his buns off. I got a thrill out of listening to him play at all times. Of course, he didn't play quite as well as in the forties and fifties, but he still played better than anyone around.

'In the last two or three years, I was with him almost daily. I'd be banging on the piano and doing finger exercises from the book and Bud would be sitting in his chair and laughing at me, tears coming out of his eyes.'

Johnny Griffin made his first recordings in Europe at the Warsaw Philharmonic Hall on October 26th and 27th 1963, when he performed with Kenny Drew, Ruud Jacobs, Wim Overgaauw and drummer Robert Joseph in the Jazz Jamboree event. The album, *Jazz Jamboree '63*, was released on the Polish Muza label.

In December 1963, Johnny returned to Ronnie Scott's Club for another four-week engagement, again backed by Stan Tracey, Malcolm Cecil and Jackie Dougan. Some of the numbers from this engagement were recorded and released, under the title *Live in London*, on Harkit Records. And in Cologne on February 13th 1964, Johnny made his first album with Kenny Clarke – *Night Lady* – for the Philips label, with Francy Boland on piano and Jimmy Woode on bass.

When Griffin left the Blue Note early in 1964, Kenny Clarke returned to the club and teamed up with organist Lou Bennett, guitarist Jimmy Gourley and bassist Jimmy Woode.

'At this time,' says Johnny, 'I didn't hang out with Klook a lot because I worked mostly with Arthur Taylor in clubs such as Le Chat Qui Pêche and the Club St. Germain. Sometimes, though, I'd go out to Kenny's house and cook and then we'd sit in the backyard and talk. I got closer to him when we went on vacation together. I talked a lot with Klook then. He took a great interest in what was going on in the world – he always had his head in newspapers and would listen regularly to the news on the radio.'

On March 13th 1964, the Hot Club de Paris, with the support of Francis Paudras and the magazine *Jazz Hot*, organized a benefit concert for Bud Powell to raise money to pay his hospital bills. This *Grand Festival Mondial en Hommage à Bud Powell* was held at the Salle Wagram and featured a host of French and American jazzmen. Apart from Johnny Griffin, the list including Hazel Scott, René Urtreger, Donald Byrd, Mae Mercer, Art Taylor, George Arvanitas, Art Simmons, Jean-Luc Ponty, Gilbert 'Bibi' Rovere, Henri Renaud and Roger Guérin.

In the spring of 1964, Johnny Griffin met up with Anders Stefansen, a producer with the Copenhagen-based jazz record company, Storyville, who was spending a couple of weeks in Paris and checking out the jazz club scene. Storyville, Europe's oldest independent jazz label, which was named after the notorious New Orleans red light district, was founded by Karl-Emil Knudsen in 1950.

Johnny asked Stefansen what chance he thought there might be of his playing an engagement in the Montmartre Jazzhus in Copenhagen and Stefansen promised to look into the possibilities.

Storyville Records' Anders Stefansen (*left*) with Johnny Griffin and Art Taylor in the Café de Flore, Paris. It was soon after this meeting that Johnny and Art made their debut at the Montmartre Jazzhus, Copenhagen, in June 1964 (photo Vibeke Gundelund).

The Jazzhus Montmartre, which first opened in the late 1950s, was the No. 1 Scandinavian jazz club and one of the most enterprising jazz venues in Europe. It was certainly a major factor in the renaissance of the Danish jazz scene, which began in the early 1960s. Founded by Anders Dyrup, a partner of Karl-Emil Knudsen in the Jazz Jamboree concert agency, the Jazzhus was initially located on Dahlerupsgade, but later moved to Store Regnegade, where it came under the management of Herluf Kamp-Larsen and Per Svensson.

On his return to Copenhagen, Anders Stefansen contact-ed Kamp-Larsen regarding an engagement for Johnny Griffin. Since it was the policy at the Montmartre to hire top musicians from the USA, sometimes for weeks at a time, Kamp-Larsen was only too happy to book the Little Giant to play in the Jazzhus in June, along with Kenny Drew (now based in Copenhagen), Niels Henning Ørsted Pedersen and Art Taylor, who came up from Paris with Johnny to take over the drum chair from the house man, Alex Riel.

Masters of Jazz Volume 7: Storyville compilation recorded in Copenhagen's Montmartre and Slukefter clubs in 1964, 1984 and 1989 (produced by Anders Stefansen, cover photo David Redfern).

In addition to bringing over musicians from the States, the Montmartre Jazzhus was able to book such distinguished local residents as Stan Getz and Oscar Pettiford, both of whom had relocated to Copenhagen in 1958, and, later, Dexter Gordon, Ben Webster, Duke Jordan, Horace Parlan, Ed Thigpen and Thad Jones.

* * *

In August 1964, Francis Paudras accompanied Bud Powell to Edenville on the Normandy coast, where Bud played a seven-day engagement at the Hotel-Restaurant la Belle Escale, with bassist Guy Hayat and drummer Jacques Gervais. Johnny Griffin, who had no engagements at this time, was invited to guest with the trio. He happily accepted and journeyed to Edenville to join Bud Powell. Recordings from this engagement were released by Fontana in France, Black Lion in the UK and Mythic Sound in Italy.

Two days later, Powell returned to New York. 'The last thing he said to me before he left for the States,' says Johnny, 'was that he was afraid to go back. I told him he didn't have to. But they had booked him into Birdland, where he played with bassist John Ore and drummer J. C. Moses. And that was the beginning of the end. Francis Paudras tried repeatedly to get Bud to come back to Paris – but once he got caught up in that New York quagmire on his own, nothing could have saved him. If you know New York like I know New York, you would understand. I'm surprised he lasted so long. He just didn't care to live.'

Bud Powell died in Kings County Hospital in Brooklyn on August 1st 1966.

*   *   *

In the summer of 1965, Griffin was booked to open a new Paris club, Jazz Land, on the Left Bank. Art Taylor had returned to the States in the spring of 1964, but, at Johnny's request, he came back to Paris to complete a quartet, with Eddie Louiss on piano and Alby Cullaz on bass.

The Paris jazz club scene was booming in 1965. Reviewing the live jazz activity in the French capital for *Melody Maker* in July of that year, I noted that, as well as Griffin at Jazz Land, and Kenny Clarke, Nathan Davis, Jimmy Gourley, Jimmy

Woode and René Urtreger at the Blue Note, jazz fans could see Art Simmons and Aaron Bridgers at the Living Room; Don Cherry at Le Chat Qui Pêche; Jack Butler and Benny Waters at La Cigale; Mae Mercer at the Trois Mailletz; Maxim Saury at the Caveau de la Huchette, and stride pianist Joe Turner at La Calavados.

Jazz Land was in the 5th arrondissement, located in the Grande Severine building, at No. 7, rue Saint-Severin, near the St. Michel Métro station. The rue Saint-Severin was also the location of the offices of the notorious Olympia Press, founded by Maurice Girodias in 1953. Girodias had published Vladimir Nabokov's *Lolita* in 1955. He also published William Burroughs' *The Naked Lunch*, Dominique Aury's *The Story of O* and works by the Marquis De Sade and Henry Miller. With the money he made from *Lolita,* he opened a three-floor entertainment complex, La Grande Severine, in a building next door to his editorial offices. It included a Parisian night-club, a Russian cabaret room (Chez Vodka), a Brazilian club (Batucada) a jazz club (the Blues Bar) and a theatre.

Reviewing Johnny's performance on the opening night at the Jazz Land club for *Melody Maker* in July 1965, I wrote:

'Johnny Griffin's arrival in Paris to open a new jazz club on the Left Bank has injected new life into what had become a rather sad scene. The club – Jazz Land – is currently the most swinging place in the French capital and on opening night it was standing room only.

'What was to have been the bandstand is, in fact, occupied by tables and chairs – Griffin had the piano moved down among the audience. "You get a better atmosphere that way," he told me. "This is a great scene and we just hope it makes it. I can tell you, they are paying me plenty. I'm very happy to be here with Art."

'And this happiness was reflected in his playing. He has never played better and the support from Art Taylor, Alby Cullaz and Eddie Louiss left nothing to be desired. All of the old Griffin characteristics were there – the long, searing, searching phrases, often repeated a semitone up, the shrill high-note crotchet trailing off down the scale in a flurry of quavers, the humour, the slightly bent quotes. And it was a delight to hear again the hissing insistency of Taylor's rivet cymbal, impeccably on the beat, driving chorus after chorus towards a super-heated climax.

'Cullaz, one of the two musician sons of French jazz critic Maurice Cullaz, is a sensitive and accurate bass player who is undaunted by some of the furious Griffin tempos, and Louiss plays a good piano, although he wasn't particularly well served by the baby grand which was lacking in volume and had several treble notes badly out of tune.

'Guests who looked in on opening night included Steve Lacy, fresh from a month in Copenhagen, and veteran clarinettist Albert Nicholas.'

* * *

It was in the second week of July 1965 that Griffin was contacted by the French pianist, composer and arranger, Raymond Fol, and invited to take part in a recording of his 'jazzed up' arrangement of Antonio Vivaldi's *The Four Seasons*. The recording, for the Philips label, took place in Paris between July 9th and 15th and involved a twenty-seven-piece ensemble, which included, in addition to Griffin, trumpeters Yvan Julian and Roger Guérin, trombonists Raymond Katarzynski and Charles Verstraete, tenor saxophonist Dominique Chanson, vibraphonist Fats Sadi, guitarist Pierre Cullaz, bassist Jimmy Woode, drummer Arthur Taylor and percussionist Jean-Louis Viale, with Raymond Fol on piano and celeste.

'After the session,' Griffin recalls, 'I went to hear the original version of *The Four Seasons*. The next day, I telephoned Raymond Fol and told him what a genius he was to have made such beautiful arrangements out of that sad baroque music. (Excuse me, all lovers of baroque music!)'

Some weeks after its opening, Jazz Land had a visit from a twenty-year-old Dutch woman, Miriam Verhaar, a secretary and part-time model for a British fashion company based in Amsterdam. She had come to Paris with a friend for a short vacation. She knew nothing about jazz, had no interest in the music, but her friend wanted to go to the Jazz Land club to meet some people he knew.

When she came into the club, Johnny Griffin was in full solo flight; but, suddenly, all his attention was focused not on the music but on the new arrival. Miriam also fixed her gaze on the Little Giant – and, as they say in France, it was *un coup de foudre* – love at first sight.

Recalling that magic moment, Miriam says:

'As soon as I saw Johnny Griffin on the stage. I fell in love.'

And Johnny recalls: 'I was completely captivated when I saw her. Couldn't take my eyes off her. It really was love at first sight.'

A short time later, Miriam gave up her job and left Holland to live with Johnny, who was staying at the Hotel Rotary in the rue Vintimille, close to the Moulin Rouge, in the 9th arondissement. They found a furnished third-floor apartment in a rather grand large house (a type known in Paris as an *hôtel particulier*) in the rue Agar, close to the Maison de la Radio in the 16th arrondissement. And that's when the phone calls started.

* * *

When I interviewed Johnny Griffin for *Crescendo Magazine* in September 1965, I noted that: 'Ardent, well-to-do and middle-aged Frenchmen who telephone a certain number in Passy these days in the confident expectation of exchanging a few passionate phrases with their chérie, are somewhat dismayed to be answered by a man speaking English with an American accent.

'The voice belongs to that pint-sized giant of the tenor saxophone, Johnny Griffin. For he moved into the furnished apartment when the much-visited, oft-telephoned chérie moved out.

' "One guy kept on telephoning and every time I answered, he rang off. He must have been speechless with admiration for my stamina!" said Johnny.

'Thirty-seven-year-old, Chicago-born Johnny Griffin, currently resident with his quartet at the Jazz Land Club, is one of the best things to have happened to the Paris jazz scene in years.

'His declared philosophy of life is engagingly simple: "I like to feel good" – and it comes through, loud and clear, in everything he does.'

In the same interview, Johnny declared that he had left the States to come to Europe in December 1962 because he needed a change: 'Though I didn't realize how much I needed it until I went back to the States in March '63. I'd had such a great time in Europe that I came back in May that year and I've been here ever since.'

I asked what he thought of the current state of jazz. 'Deplorable,' he said, without a hint of hesitation. 'But there's nothing new about that. Eddie Davis and I used to talk about this a lot five years ago – promoters and club owners with minds like computers, musicians angry with the public because they don't get the respect they deserve, the tremendous social pressures – for white people as well as black – clubs closing down, everybody pessimistic. Then you have the market flooded with too many mediocre records.'

And he added a typically Griffinesque postscript: 'Of which I have contributed many. But the real problem is that jazz musicians are not respected. Except for a few jazz enthusiasts, people link jazz musicians with gin mills, smoky dives and so on. Musicians don't get credit for having dignity – so they tend to get back at the general public by treating them as peasants. I used to do this myself – but it's a mistake. If you get a cold audience, you don't ignore them. You've got to warm them up. If I feel a draught when I'm on the stand, then I know I've just got to burn them down, set 'em on fire. I'll exhaust them with a real fast blues – it'll exhaust me, too, but *they'll* get warm watching *me* get warm. I'll just blast 'em down.'

In the mid-1960s, Johnny was very happy to have a regular club job in Paris, which paid him enough to give him the power to choose the kind of engagements he accepted outside club hours. He grinned: 'Baby, I'm a hard man to do business with when I've got a hundred dollars in my pocket!'

When Stuff Smith's illness left an unexpected gap in the Antibes Jazz Festival programme earlier in 1965, Johnny was asked to fill it with his quartet. 'They offered me $800 for two concerts. I told them I wanted more than that for myself alone. They said that I ought to "think French". That was a laugh – with me living in the most expensive city in the world. Then they told me how much all the other musicians were costing them. They had a fixed budget. So I asked them, "What about my budget?" But they wouldn't pay what I asked – so no Antibes. Man, it's a good position to be in.

And you can bet that if I ever take time off from the club to play somewhere else, it'll be because I'm getting a heap of money for it.

'You know, booking agents always try to kid musicians that they are doing them a favour. That's crazy. The musicians are doing the agents a favour – because they live on the commission they charge the promoters or club owners. They just sit on their fat fannies talking into a telephone and getting rich.'

In the same interview, I asked Johnny about his recording plans:

'I hate making records,' he said. 'Those cold studios – all those mikes and cables and technicians. They stand me by a mike and tell me not to move – but man, I *like* to move when I play. I just wish someone could record the quartet without us knowing. Wait a minute – just forget I said that!

'In the States, musicians do too many records they don't really want to make – just for the money. And, even then, the money is rarely good enough. I did a lot of records like that.'

'Are you happy with all of your albums?' I asked.

'Yeah. *The Change of Pace* album (February 1961) with two bass players (Bill Lee and Larry Gales) was good. And I liked *The Big Soul Band* one (May 1960), too. The band was a bit sloppy, but we had a good feeling going. I also liked the *Tough Tenors* album (November 1960), with Eddie Davis. That rhythm section (Junior Mance, piano; Larry Gales, bass; Ben Riley, drums) really swung. Then the *Full House* one (June 1962) with Wes Montgomery was a happy date – there was an audience on that one and it makes a lot of difference.'

Johnny was in no hurry to return to the States. But he would take issue with you if you described him as an exile. 'I don't really feel like an exile. I've always had the feeling, anyway, that I'm from another planet.'

On December 11th, 1969, when Art Taylor interviewed Johnny Griffin for his book, *Notes And Tones*, the following exchange would take place:

Johnny Griffin: I'm not really from this planet. I did something wrong on my planet and they sent me here to pay my dues. I figure pretty soon my dues should be paid. And they'll call me back home so I can rest in peace.

Art Taylor: You're not serious about that, are you?

Johnny Griffin: I can't be from this place, Arthur. There is no love here and I love people. All I see is hate around me, except for a few of my friends. That's what's wrong with the earth today. Black and white on this planet, there is no love, there is only hate. I was thinking about reading some books on anarchy, because all this government stuff is b. s. anyway. These governments drawing lines between men, tribes between tribes. Yellow people against brown people against black against Muslims against Christians against Hindus. What is all of that? I know I'm not from this planet. I can't be. I must be from some place else in the universe, because I'm a total misfit. I can't get with none of this.

'I like to wander around, meet new people,' he told me in 1965. 'You get sick of the same club, the same faces, the same complaints. It's boring. I stopped having fun when I went on the gig – so it was time to quit. Everything was so negative, with everybody putting down everybody else. As I said, I believe in feeling good – and, in Paris, I feel good. And I like to help other people feel good, too.'

When asked what he thought about the avant-garde scene at that time in the States, he replied:

'I don't like the sounds, though I like some of the themes. You know, the saxophone was a buffoon instrument before

Coleman Hawkins legitimized it and earned it respect. Now these guys are putting it back in the buffoon category. The material Ornette Coleman writes is beautiful – but the sound. Ugh! It's just a sign of the times I suppose. This is what they feel – and they're expressing it. But I don't feel like that. There's so much agony in their music. I know what they mean – it is what I was feeling down the back of my neck in the States.

'The whole society is really something else. The pressures are too much. But I can't stand to hear this agony in music. The melodies are OK, but when they go into solos, you can cancel me. All this "sounds of suffering" bit. I don't need to be reminded. I've heard enough. I like to listen to sentimental music – though I play loud and boisterous myself.' Then, with a characteristically flippant afterthought, Griffin added with a grin: 'But I don't want to listen to music that excites me. I'm a nervous wreck already!'

Johnny, who said he didn't practise as much as he should, was then studying the piano intensively. He also wanted to compose more. 'But I have to be in a writing groove. Normally, I hate even to write my name – unless it's to endorse a cheque.'

Finally, I asked him what he thought about the famous gap that is supposed to exist between American and European jazz musicians – insisting that he didn't have to be indulgent just because he was talking to a European.

'That gap is getting almost non-existent with the interchange and interplay that's going on now. Ronnie Stephenson is one of the greatest drummers in the world. I mean that. And Stan Tracey has a fantastic conception. Then you have great tenor players like Ronnie Scott and Tubby Hayes and Dick Morrissey. And there's Jimmy Deuchar, the rascal.

There are also some fine big band musicians like Johnny Scott, Ronnie Ross, Johnny Dankworth.

'There's a hell of a lot of great studio musicians – man, they can see round the corner. And they can all write arrangements. You know, with all that great talent, it's such a shame that there's only one real jazz club – Ronnie Scott's – in a city the size of London. That's terrible, man, terrible.'

The telephone bell sounded the end of the interview. Some distraught Frenchman was getting desperate about chérie's sex change.

* * *

Miriam and Johnny stayed in the rue Agar apartment for several years. 'Early on,' Miriam recalls, 'while Johnny was still at the Jazz Land club, I didn't always go with him to the club because it was too tiring. So I would stay at home – and then these telephone calls would start, with men asking to speak to Christine. When I told them there was no Christine in the building, they would say, "Oh, that's OK, we'll take you." Oh, my God! I was so scared that I called Johnny at the club and he told me to order a cab and come to the club. I told him I didn't dare walk out of the house because there were some American soldiers on the second floor and they were always leaving the door open, so anyone could get into the building. So Johnny waited for the intermission and then came and picked me up and took me to the club.'

Over the subsequent weeks, the calls became less frequent and then finally stopped. But then the owners of the apartments decided to sell the building, so Miriam and Johnny had to seek alternative accommodation.

However, the cost of apartments in central Paris was so prohibitive that they decided to move to the suburbs, which Miriam hated. They took a twelfth floor apartment in

Châtillon-sous-Bagneux, a commune in the southwestern suburbs, four and a half miles from the centre of Paris.

It was during the period of Johnny Griffin's residence at the Jazz Land club, in December 1965, that he was badly injured in a road accident on his way home from the gig in the early hours of the morning. On December 12th, 1965, I sent the following report to *Down Beat* magazine:

'The combination of rain-greased roads, French traffic and an unyielding windscreen nearly robbed the world of yet another virtuoso jazz musician on December 3rd.

'Johnny Griffin, following his regular gig at the Jazz Land club in Paris, was making for the Living Room and the Art Simmons Trio at 3 a.m. when the car, driven by his French bassist, Alby Cullaz, ran smack into another vehicle at a road junction.

'Griffin's head went through the windscreen. He sustained cuts to the face and neck and was rushed to hospital for stitches to be inserted into a neck wound. His lip was also cut and he was expected to be out of action for at least a week. Drummer Art Taylor, who was also in the car, and Cullaz, escaped with bruises.'

* * *

That report ended with a reference to a 'phantom' Johnny Griffin record session. It noted that on the day before the accident (December 2nd 1965), Johnny Griffin had been a key man in a recording session for Clover Records featuring the Los Angeles singer, Kitty White. The record date had been arranged by the American millionairess and jazz enthusiast, Doris Duke, only daughter of tobacco and electric power mogul, James Duke. At this time Doris, who had inherited an $80 million fortune on the death of her father when she was thirteen, was married to pianist Joe Castro, the owner of

Clover Records. Pianist Art Simmons had arranged a dozen numbers for the date and, according to my report, musicians taking part included, as well as Johnny Griffin: Dexter Gordon, Nathan Davis, Jimmy Woode and Kenny Clarke. However there have long been conflicting accounts of just who took part in this session. According to Tom Lord's *The Jazz Discography*, the backing group included Sonny Grey (trumpet), Melih Gurel (flugel horn), Johnny Griffin, Dexter Gordon and Hal Singer (tenor saxophones), Jean-Louis Chautemps (baritone saxophone), Art Simmons (piano), Pierre Cullaz (guitar), Jimmy Woode or Michel Gaudry (bass) and Kenny Clarke (drums). Conducting duties were reported to be shared between the blues singer, Charles 'Big' Jones, and Art Simmons.

To this day, I don't know what was the source of the information for that news item I sent to *Down Beat*, but I do know that Johnny Griffin, Dexter Gordon and Hal Singer were not involved in the recording – but tenor saxophonist Nathan Davis certainly was, as he has confirmed to me.

Art Simmons is emphatic that Johnny Griffin, Dexter Gordon and Hal Singer were not on the date, but confirms that 'Big' Jones did take part in the session, along with Sonny Grey, Nathan Davis, Jimmy Woode and Kenny Clarke.

* * *

Some three years after his move to France, I interviewed Johnny for *Melody Maker* and discovered that, although he was extremely happy with the relaxed lifestyle and cultural environment he enjoyed in Paris, he planned to return to the United States at some time in the future to check out the jazz scene and team up with some of his former associates. As I noted in the *Melody Maker* of March 16th 1966:

'If Johnny Griffin were as good a doctor, novelist, chef or jockey as he is a tenor player, he would command a good deal more respect – and certainly a great deal more money – than he does at this precise moment.

'It is one of the gratuitous hazards of life as a jazz musician that, even when you are brilliant at your job, the work is irregular, the rewards inadequate and your popularity with the public as fluctuating as a belly dancer's navel.

'By any standards, Johnny Griffin is a superb musician; yet you will look in vain for his name in the tenor saxophone section of the recent *Melody Maker* polls.'

I reported that he was then 'cooling his heels in a Paris flat', working very occasionally and recording not at all. He was, he said, living on the end of his capital. And he added, with a grin, that he needed a lot of money because he had expensive tastes:

'Sometimes,' he said, 'I get depressed and ask myself why I didn't become a doctor or a lawyer, or something. They have big homes, plenty of money. But the mood doesn't last long. There's really nothing else for me to be.

'In the States sometimes, when things were slack, my family would get on to me to get a job. I'd go to IBM or the gas company or the post office and fill in an application form. OK, they'd say, you can start tomorrow – and that would scare the hell out of me.

'A jazz musician's life can be tough, but the compensations are priceless. To be able to express yourself through music – that's wonderful. I don't regret a single day of my life as a musician.'

Johnny stated that he liked the relaxed atmosphere of Europe and enjoyed the greater individual freedom, but had never entertained the illusion that American jazzmen could make their fortunes in Europe:

'Of course, I could earn much more money in the States. But man, that rat race! At one time I used to thrive on it – but it finally brought me down.

'I remember opening at a gig in New York and the atmosphere on the stand was terrible – cold, really chilly. The first night, the pianist didn't turn up, the bass player was loaded to his eyes and the drummer was kicking his dope habit on the stand.

'I've worked as a professional musician since I was fourteen. Most of the jobs I had around Chicago were for gangsters, but they were always good to musicians.'

Johnny had plans at that time to return to the States eventually. 'I'll just have to go back – but I certainly hope the atmosphere will be better. Meanwhile, I'm still practising and playing the way I want to play.'

My view, expressed in the report of this interview in 1966, was that 'since the way Johnny Griffin likes to play is one of the best ways of playing tenor I know, it's a pity he's not playing more often.'

* * *

Towards the end of 1965, pressure was being put on club owners by the Paris branch of the musicians' union (*syndicat*) as the Paris colony of self-exiled American musicians began to expand – because working opportunities for French musicians became increasingly limited. The *syndicat* wanted a quota. Whereas in 1930 there had been seven thousand professional musicians working in the Paris region, the number had now dwindled to less than two thousand, the majority of whom were without regular work. The *syndicat* sent a letter to twenty-five club owners.

Hardly anyone was aware of it, but, from 1933, there had been a law in France that the percentage of foreign musicians in any group should not exceed ten. That meant that practically every jazz club in Paris was in breach of the law.

'So now it's "Yanks go home!",' said singer 'Big' Jones. 'But who is the French tenor player who is going to pull in the people like Johnny Griffin does?'

From the mid-1960s onwards, Griffin worked more widely in Europe, with dates in Germany, Poland, Yugoslavia, Italy and Spain – and quite regularly in Scandinavia. He says, 'I'd go up to Copenhagen, pick up Kenny Drew, Niels-Henning Ørsted Pedersen and Albert Heath, play a month in the Montmartre Jazzhus in Copenhagen and then play at the Golden Circle in Stockholm and the Metropol in Oslo for a week or two.'

On March 30th and 31st 1967, all of his sets at the Jazzhus, with Kenny Drew, Niels-Henning Ørsted Pedersen and Albert Heath, were recorded, resulting in three albums – *The Man I Love* for Alan Bates' Black Lion label, and *A Night in Tunisia* and *You Leave Me Breathless* for Bates' Freedom label. And at the same venue, in July 1973, he recorded *Blues for Harvey*, with Kenny Drew, Mads Vinding and Ed Thigpen for the Danish SteepleChase label.

Blues for Harvey was Griffin's tribute to Harvey Sand, a dedicated jazz fan with a wild sense of humour, who worked as a waiter and barman at the Jazzhus Montmartre and who befriended all the musicians who appeared at the club. According to Anders Stefansen of Storyville, Harvey was, at one time, employed as a handy man at the Atlantic cinema in Copenhagen. It was his practice, when the feature film was shorter than usual, to augment the advertised programmeme by running the short feature film, *Jammin' the Blues*, a 1944

Art Taylor (drums), Björn Pedersen (bass), Kenny Drew (piano) and Johnny Griffin at the Metropol Hotel, Oslo, 1965 (photo Randi Hultin).

production directed by Gjon Mili, which featured Lester Young, Harry Edison, Illinois Jacquet, Barney Kessel, Red Callender and Jo Jones, among others. Some years later, when Johnny was announcing the title tune of the *Blues for Harvey* album during a gig in a New York Club, he told the audience, 'This number is dedicated to a very good friend of mine who helped me when I was in medical need – he was a barman in Copenhagen.'

* * *

Booze for Harvey! Johnny and his 'medical helper', Harvey Sand, in Copenhagen.

On September 12th 1968, Miriam and Johnny celebrated a happy event when Miriam gave birth to their daughter, Cynthia. The following year Johnny divorced Joan, his first wife, and on November 15th he and Miriam were married at the Mairie of Chatillon-sous-Bagneux. The guests included Memphis Slim, Hank Mobley, Arthur Taylor and Sidney Bechet's widow, Jacqueline.

Says Miriam, 'Now that we had a daughter, it became more important than ever to move from that 12th floor apartment. We tried to find a house near Paris but without success. Then, one day, my father called me and said he had found a nice property for sale in Bergambacht, Holland. I went to look at it, liked it and decided to move in. Johnny stayed behind in Paris for a couple of months, organizing the transportation of what little furniture we had to Holland. Then he joined me in the new home, where we were to stay for the next seven years.'

12

The Clarke–Boland
Big Band

The Kenny Clarke–Francy Boland Big Band was, by far, the finest jazz orchestra ever assembled outside the United States. It was the brainchild of a German-born Italian socialist, architect and jazz lover, Pier-Luigi Campi, who ran a flourishing coffee bar in Cologne's Hohestrasse.

As I noted at the time of the band's formation, its leaders were two musicians who competed with each other in the art of staying in the background and maintaining a low profile.[8]

In the course of its eleven years of existence, this multinational orchestra made a massive impact on the European jazz scene with outstanding recordings and live appearances throughout the continent. Its roster of members over the years embraced more than a dozen nationalities and half-a-dozen religions and its performances were eloquent testimony to the impressive strides European jazzmen had made in catching up with their American counterparts.

The band's début album, *Jazz is Universal*, for the Atlantic label, was recorded in Cologne on December 13th 1961. Holding their own in the line-up with Americans Benny Bailey, Nat Peck, Zoot Sims, Sahib Shihab and Jimmy

Woode, were Roger Guérin from France, Jimmy Deuchar and Derek Humble from Britain, Ahmed Muvaffak Falay from Turkey, Åke Persson from Sweden and Carl Drewo from Austria. In the liner note for the album, Voice of America producer and presenter Willis Conover wrote:

'The thoroughly integrated sound that emerged from this band is convincing evidence that international boundaries have no meaning at all to the practising jazz musician.'

On May 16th 1963, a couple of days before catching the boat to Rotterdam with Babs Gonzales, Johnny Griffin had completed a two-day recording session in New York for Atlantic Records. The album, *Soul Groove*, featured Matthew Gee (trombone), Aaron Bell (bass, tuba), John Patton (organ), Hank Jones (piano), Art Taylor (drums) and Carlos 'Patato' Valdes (conga and bongos). Before he left the studio, Griffin was given a copy of *Jazz is Universal* and that was his first introduction to the Clarke–Boland Big Band.

Early in 1964, Siegfried Loch, jazz label manager for Philips, approached Gigi Campi with a proposal that Johnny Griffin be invited to Cologne to record an album with the rhythm section of the Clarke–Boland Big Band: Francy Boland, Jimmy Woode and Kenny Clarke. Campi agreed and contacted Johnny, who was immensely enthusiastic about the idea. On February 13th 1964, Griffin arrived in Cologne and met Campi and the illustrious rhythm section in the EMI recording studios.

The album that resulted from this session, *Night Lady*, was a veritable gem, especially noteworthy for the sublime compatibility that existed among the four musicians. 'It was a dream to work with that rhythm section,' says Johnny. And it was no surprise that, when he was invited to join the saxophone section of the Clarke–Boland Big Band, some four

Left to right: Kenny Clarke, Gigi Campi and Francy Boland, July 1967.

years later, as a replacement for Billy Mitchell, he accepted with alacrity.

Regular work with a big band had not been on the Griffin agenda since he left the Lionel Hampton band back in May 1947. But when he was called to join the C–BBB in Cologne, he didn't think twice: 'I took the train from Paris to Cologne with Klook and joined Ronnie Scott, Derek Humble, Carl Drewo and Sahib Shihab in the saxophone section.' And he remained a regular member of the band for the next two years. 'Once I got in the band,' he told me, with typical Griffin humour, 'they couldn't get rid of me.'

In a 1974 interview with *Melody Maker*'s Max Jones, Johnny said that playing with the Clarke–Boland Big Band was one of the most fantastic experiences he had ever had. 'The musicianship in the band was of such a high level to begin with.

And the ambience of that band, the spirit among the musicians themselves – it was beautiful. Then there was the music that Francy wrote; it was different, totally different, from anything I was used to. Yes, it was some experience.'

And Johnny told me, in an April 1997 interview:

'It was a truly superb ensemble. Working with that band is one of my happiest musical memories. I was amazed how these great musicians, with their inflated egos, got on so well together. That was a band full of bandleaders, lions, tigers and gorillas! Yet there was so little friction. Usually in a big band there are factions that develop. This was the case with the Duke Ellington band and with the Lionel Hampton band. In Duke's band, cats didn't speak to each other for twenty-five years. And I couldn't understand how the hell they could make such beautiful music when some of them hated each other. But when they got on the bandstand with the maestro, it was all beautiful music.

'But with the C–BBB it was different. Francy was the least likely bandleader I had ever met in my life. But the guys had so much respect for him – so there was never a case of harsh words or disciplinary action. He was humble, mild-mannered and soft-spoken and he controlled those brutes. I was amazed. Look at Art Farmer, Benny Bailey and Idrees Sulieman – three Leos right there. Can you imagine? Three Leo trumpeters – and all of them stars! But they got along.

'And the saxophone section was terrific. All the musicians were fantastic. Derek Humble was a superb lead alto player and a hell of a soloist. I never played with a better lead alto than Derek. He played the instrument like it was a tenor – the power that he had. He made it seem so easy.

'There was no weak spot in that band. There were no passengers – they were all executives. And with Francy Boland

Griffin (*left*) with Kenny Clarke, taking a break with the Clarke–Boland Big Band (photo Heinz Bähr, courtesy Campi Archive).

doing practically all of the writing, it had a distinctive, characteristic sound. The quality of the music was definitely a factor in keeping the band together. What really made that band so special was the great respect the musicians had for Kenny and Francy and for each other – the guys would listen to each other, that's why the section work was so good. The Clarke–Boland Big Band couldn't have lasted with a Benny Goodman or a Buddy Rich leading it – because there were too many bandleaders in the band. It just wouldn't have worked if the leaders had been dictators.

'What also struck me was that there were so many different styles of improvisation. I was amazed by Tony Coe. His clarinet reminded me so much of Barney Bigard – that big

CD insert for the Clarke–Boland Big Band: *The Verve Collection*, reissuing the LPs *All Blues* (recorded 1968) and *Sax No End* (1967). The trombone player at the front is Åke Persson; Johnny Griffin is on his right.

round sound – and his saxophone reminded me of Paul Gonsalves and Lucky Thompson. Francy Boland had very delicate touch – like Ahmad Jamal. Instead of hammering the piano like Bud, he would get a bell sound out of the instrument. Trombonist Åke Persson was another giant, a highly individualistic player, and Nat Peck was also a major force in that section – he'd had so much experience with the Glenn Miller band. And don't forget Ronnie Scott – a great tenor saxophonist – and two highly distinctive trumpet players in Benny Bailey and Art Farmer.

'It was in 1968 that I really got close to Klook. We had a vacation together in the south of France. He had great integrity as a musician and real dignity as a man. He was a perfect gentleman with impeccable manners. And he was always well-dressed. He was always able to see the humour in a situation, which made him better able to make his way through life. He was a very positive person – but when certain things bothered him, he would draw the line and let you know in no uncertain terms. He could get very angry sometimes – but always in a calm way – like a Sicilian, never loud, but whistling through his teeth – and you could sense the danger ahead!

'Like me, Klook liked to have a good time and feel good. He liked to laugh and smile and tell jokes. But he was pretty conservative. He was not a big drinker and he never used bad language. At the drums, he was like a kid playing with his toys. What made him such a distinctive drummer was his attack, the real crispness of his playing, the way he used the snare drum and his top cymbal sound. His time was impeccable. Rock steady. And then there was the way he'd drop his bombs – sometimes instead of doing it on the first beat, he'd do it on the second.

'Kenny was a hell of a musician and, without doubt, the foremost innovator of modern drumming. He wasn't the world's greatest technician, he didn't have the fluency of Philly Joe Jones – who was the greatest drummer I ever worked with – but his time was impeccable and he knew the drums from A to Z

'You know, everyone in the Clarke–Boland band would hang with Kenny. They all had great respect for him. Sometimes, when the guys started acting up, he would put his foot down. He would say something quietly, but firmly, and when he did that, everybody would cool it.'

* * *

On June 18th 1967, Johnny Griffin made his first recording with the C–BBB – *Sax No End* – for the German SABA label (which later became MPS). The session re-united him with his old Tough Tenors partner, Lockjaw Davis, who is featured on five of the eight numbers, most notably on the title track, a ground-breaking arrangement by Francy Boland. This saxophone soli masterpiece, based on the chords of 'Chinatown', was a major landmark in the band's progress towards its ultimate corporate identity. With Johnny in the saxophone section were Derek Humble (alto sax), Carl Drewo and Ronnie Scott (tenor saxes), and Sahib Shihab (baritone sax). For the date, Francy Boland's original composition, 'Major's Groove', was re-titled 'Griff's Groove' and included as a special feature for Johnny Griffin.

Griffin's last reunion with Jaws occurred in November 1983, when the Tough Tenors had a one-week engagement in New York's Blue Note, with Donald Brown on piano, Curtis Lundy on bass and Kenny Washington on drums. Eddie Davis died of cancer on September 3rd 1986. Johnny had visited him in Culver City, California, just a few days earlier. Says Johnny, 'His death hit me very hard. He was one of my favourite tenor players. Our styles were so divergent – radically opposite ends of the pole, just as our characters were, on the outside. But Jaws was like an older brother for me and he will be sorely missed in the music world.'

On August 27th 1968, Johnny joined Benny Bailey, Åke Persson, Sahib Shihab, Francy Boland, Woode, Klook and Kenny Clare for a session in the EMI Studios in Cologne which produced five tracks: 'Foot Patting', 'Please Send Me Someone to Love', 'Deep Eight', 'The JAMFs Are Coming', and 'Lady Heavy Bottom's Waltz'. Johnny insists that the last track did not refer to any corpulent colleen in particular.

The Clarke–Boland Big Band at the Venice Casino during the Venice Film Festival, 1969. *Back row*: Idrees Sulieman, Tony Fisher, Dusko Goykovich; *middle row*: Nat Peck, Åke Persson, Erik van Lier; *front row*: Johnny Griffin, Tubby Hayes (replacing Ronnie Scott on this occasion); *standing in front, soloing*: Benny Bailey; (photo Heinz Bähr, Gigi Campi Archive).

The session was Gigi Campi's idea, but the titles were not released until three decades later in a two-LP, sixteen-track compilation, *Griff 'n' Bags*, on the Italian Rearward label. The record also featured Milt Jackson on five numbers recorded on February 2nd 1969, with Shihab, Boland, Woode and Clarke. The idea had originally been to have Milt 'Bags' Jackson reunited with his former Modern Jazz Quartet drummer for a big band album, but this plan never came to fruition.

On February 17th 1969, the Clarke–Boland Big Band began a two-week engagement at Ronnie Scott's in London that set a new attendance record for the club. This was the first time that the band had played together for more than five consecutive days and that memorable fortnight, to quote sleevenote writer John Legg, 'helped the band achieve a perfect unison.' Happily, the band recorded two albums for the Polydor label during this engagement and those thirteen tracks represent what is widely regarded as the band's best recorded work.

'It was marvellous,' said Ronnie Scott. 'People used to applaud in the middle of the arrangements. It was one of the greatest musical experiences of my life.'

However, on the opening Monday night, Johnny Griffin was missing from the saxophone section because he was spending the night in Pentonville prison. He and the band arrived at the club at around 6 pm and, while the musicians were setting up, one of the club staff came to Johnny and told him that there were three bailiffs asking to see him. He went to the entrance to meet them and was told that he was being arrested for contempt of court.

'I couldn't believe it,' says Johnny. 'They told me I hadn't paid the tax that was due on the money I'd received for a gig in England six or seven months earlier. I told them that I'd paid the tax to the UK agency that booked me, but apparently the agency hadn't passed it on to the Inland Revenue. The bailiffs told me that they had no option but to take me to prison.'

Johnny was then escorted to Pentonville prison, where he underwent a gruelling ordeal:

'The first thing that happened was that I got stripped and then put into a tub of hot water – which was scalding. Then I was taken to the doctor who asked me what drugs I was using. Well, at that time, I wasn't using any drugs. I'd got interested in Islam and had decided to clean up my act. I'd also stopped drinking. We had played a date in Venice some days earlier and the guys in the band couldn't believe I was on the wagon.

'The next thing that happened in Pentonville was that they told me I was in the wrong prison – that I should have been in Brixton. So they transferred me to the prison hospital in Brixton, where one of the inmates told me to be careful because the guard that brought me in was likely to be attacked by some of the prisoners because he had beaten one of them up. He said that if I was around when they came for the guard, I could be beaten up, too.

'The next morning we go down for breakfast in this big room. There is some foul-smelling fish in a big barrel, and I really couldn't make it. It wasn't a bit like the *soupe de poissons* that I'd been used to on the Côte d'Azur. One of the prisoners, an Italian who was doing time for hi-jacking a truck, saw that I wasn't too impressed. He was on a special diet, so he went to where the food was kept and brought me some milk – which was very nice of him.

'They transferred me from the hospital into the cell block where I was given a note which told me that, because I was in jail for contempt of court, I had to pay a penalty of £500, which I could work off at the rate of £1 a day – so that in a matter of 500 days, I could be out of there. Happily, though, the Ronnie Scott Club's lawyers arrived and they got me released in time to make the gig on Tuesday night. The musicians died laughing when they saw me – they really had a ball.

'I hadn't drunk a drop of alcohol for six months – but when I walked into the club that evening, the girl singer, Salena Jones, handed me a bottle of champagne – and I drank the whole bottle without taking a breath.

'It really hadn't been a very nice way for Britain to welcome a jazz musician – and I had had such happy times in London before that!'

* * *

It was Griffin's brief spell of incarceration that inspired Francy Boland to write the jazz suite, *At Her Majesty's Pleasure*, which the Clarke–Boland Big Band recorded for Black Lion in Cologne on September 5th 1969. This was Johnny's last album with the band.

As Bob Houston observed in the liner note:

'While the Kenny Clarke-Francy Boland Band were still known to a select band of fanatical listeners, the great ambition of the band's mentor, Gigi Campi, was to come to Britain, and especially the Ronnie Scott Club in London. Well, they finally made it and, as any of the increasing number of converts will tell you, the rest is history.

'But the most traumatic memories of that memorable first visit to Britain are those of tenorist Johnny Griffin. He had a rather special welcome from the law, who whisked him off to Pentonville. I must hasten to add that the chirpy Griffin had done nothing more dastardly than forget to pay some tax which Her Majesty's Inland Revenue Department were rather anxious to collect. There but for the grace of God . . .

'Anyway, our policemen being wonderful and Gigi Campi having a sufficiently large fistful of the readies, Griffin's stay in Pentonville turned out to be a mere one-night stand and he returned, triumphantly, to the C–BBB and their great Scott Club triumph.'

* * *

Following the tremendous success of that Ronnie Scott engagement, the band was back at the club in October 1970, this time for a three-week spell.

Looking back on that time, Griffin can't resist recalling an incident which, he says, exemplifies Kenny Clarke's sensitivity about the use of bad language. The band was getting ready to play Johnny's original, *The JAMFs are Coming* – in which JAMFs stands for 'Jive-Assed Mother Fuckers'.

Says Griffin, 'When Kenny announced the tune, somebody shouted, "What does JAMFs mean?" and Kenny was really embarrassed, especially because Princess Margaret was in the club that night. He looked fiercely at me and then turned back to the mike and said, "Oh, well . . . it means, er . . . it means, Just A Mere Friend." And the whole band just fell about.'

In the autumn of 1969, the Clarke-Boland Big Band made a five-concert tour with the Thad Jones–Mel Lewis Band, and Johnny Griffin recalls that the combination of these two outstanding big bands generated a tremendously enthusiastic response from the audiences.

On September 7th, the two bands played at the De Doelen concert hall in Rotterdam where, as Jan van Setten noted in the *Melody Maker*, 1,780 people exploded into thunderous acclaim after the four-and-a-half-hour marathon concert.

Wrote van Setten: 'In the last four years, the J-LBB in America and the C-BBB in Europe have rejuvenated,

Guest musicians with the Westdeutscher Rundfunk Big Band in Köln, November 6th 1999. *Left to right, standing*: bandleader John Clayton, Erik van Lier (trombone), WDR producer Wolfgang Hirschmann; *sitting*: Gigi Campi, Griffin, Billy Mitchell (tenor sax), Benny Bailey (trumpet); (photo Ines Kaiser).

restored and revived a flagging jazz scene by demonstrating, both live and on record, that the combination of high voltage enthusiasm, outstanding arrangements, virtuoso musicianship and irresistible swing, produces a brand of jazz excitement which just cannot be equalled by a small group.

'Now they were joined in battle in Rotterdam, with further contests lined up for Basle and Frankfurt; and it evoked memories of the cutting contests in American ballrooms during the golden age of the big bands . . .

'Relaxing in a band room armchair, Thad Jones said: "This tour has shown that there is a great desire by the public to hear more big band music. The response has been slightly under fantastic . . . With big bands you get that extra quality of excitement, that strong emotion and feeling."

'The Rotterdam concert was one of the most unforgettable nights of jazz I have ever had the good fortune to experience. It was a real battle of the bands. Who won? Music.'

Writing about the two big bands in the *Herald Tribune* on July 28th 2004, in an article headed *Wanted: big bands, dead or alive*, Mike Zwerin noted: 'Mel Lewis was the thinking man's big band drummer, and Jones, a trumpeter, was an extraordinarily inventive arranger and composer and a charismatic frontman.

'The most worldly big band of them all was based in Cologne and co-led by the prototype American jazzman in Paris, Kenny Clarke, and the Belgian pianist and arranger Francy Boland. The LPs *All Smiles* and *More Smiles*, originally recorded for the German label MPS in the late 1960s, have been released for the first time on CD by Verve/Europe. The sidemen, all either Europeans or Americans living in Europe, included Johnny Griffin, Sahib Shihab, and the English legend Ronnie Scott on saxophones, the Yugoslav Dusko Goykovich on trumpet, the Swedish trombonist Åke Persson, the Swiss-resident Jimmy Woode on bass and Clarke on drums. Along with Jones–Lewis, the Clarke–Boland band kept the fluttering flame burning despite rock's dominance in the 1960s and '70s.'

13

Going Dutch

In the spring of 1973, Johnny and Miriam left Paris and moved to Bergambacht, about fifteen miles from Rotterdam. There, they set up house in a converted barn. Says Johnny. 'The surrounding countryside was really beautiful – with windmills, flowers everywhere and lovely old houses.'

And talking of life in Bergambacht to Bill Moody, in an interview for his 1993 book *The Jazz Exiles*, he said that Paris was fine, but living in an apartment had been driving him crazy. 'Now, I just go out and make my gigs, then go back to this five-hundred-year-old village and relax, compose, blow my horn and tend my garden. It's a life I couldn't live over here [in America].'[9]

Tending his garden included looking after his *cannabis sativa* crop. Johnny told me, 'It was crazy – in Holland the newspapers had articles telling you how to grow marijuana, how to cultivate it. I had a crop in Holland. And if you didn't want to grow it, they'd tell you where you could buy it, different varieties.'

In June 1974, Griffin played Ronnie Scott's Club with Mike Pyne on piano, Ron Mathewson on bass and Spike Wells on drums – a rhythm section for which he had high praise. One evening, between sets, he was interviewed by Max Jones for *Melody Maker*. He was in somewhat frivolous mood – a not uncommon eventuality. Referring to the fact that so many great jazz musicians had died, he said, 'All the good musicians are dying and all the sad ones are living like crazy. Man, all those sad ones on that macrobiotic diet, they're living on. And I'm healthier than ever. No chance for me to die; I've got too much suffering to do.'

Talking about the move from France to Holland, he said he had been living in Holland, off and on, since June 1973, but only got rid of his Paris apartment in September 1973.

'If I'd stayed in France I would have moved to the country-side anyway. I was a tourist in Paris for ten years – never settled down.' And then he repeated what he had told Arthur Taylor back in 1969: 'I'm from another planet.'

He went on to tell Jones that he was thoroughly enjoying life in Holland. 'I feel like a free spirit right now, living in Europe.' He was not envisaging a return to the United States. 'But maybe I'll go and visit America. I had planned to go sometime. I really don't know. Maybe, presented with a nice opportunity for something that I'd like, where I could feel that I'd develop more, I would go back.'

When Jones asked him if that nice opportunity would involve leading his own regular group, Griffin replied that it could do and that it would be good to have such a group.

'With a steady group you can do so much more. You know, when musicians play all the time together they have an empathy for each other. It means you can really expand; you can take a theme and play for an hour with the one theme, if you really know one another. Whereas, playing with different groups, most of the time you must be careful, you must stay more on the surface of things; you cannot delve down into the core of the music.'

Max pointed out that Griffin had now been a resident of Europe for eleven years and asked if he had been home during that time.

'Home?' said Griffin, in mock surprise. 'Home? Home is where my saxophone is.' And he added that he had not been back to the States since he left there in 1963.

Jones wrote that, when pressed on the reasons for not returning to his place of origin, 'he retreated into Griffinesque humour about the American way of life, then instructed me not to "put that in" in case he wanted to return.'

'No,' said Griffin, 'I've done such terrible things that I can't go back there. But I'm sure with all the suffering I've done, they'll call me back.'

Johnny talked to Jones about life as a jazz musician. 'It is difficult at best for a jazz musician because the music itself is not subsidized and it's not pop music, although you can hear the essence of jazz in almost all commercial music on the air – I mean on programmes like detective stories – things like that. But for the real hard-core jazz musician, making a good living is difficult. For me, though, it has been very nice in Europe. That's why I've stayed. I've learned how to relax in Europe . . . to relax in my life, because it seems to me that Europeans relax more than Americans. The work drive is not so strong here; the people tend to vacation more in Europe than in America.'

Asked if American musicians living in Europe faced the prospect of running out of inspiration, because there was not the same intense competition among musicians as existed in the States, and this meant that the expatriate could become complacent or lazy, Griffin replied, 'You know, I think that after a certain point in your life as a musician, you have acquired enough experience to keep on feeding you. I left America when I was thirty-four or thirty-five years old and I feel that I had enough of the roots embedded in me, in my soul, in my life, to not have to worry about roots any more. I want to blossom; I want to grow above the earth now. To me, it's a matter of developing your mental outlook, and broadening yourself spiritually by meeting new souls and looking for new horizons.'

* * *

On April 13th 1973 Johnny Griffin was a guest soloist with a Dizzy Gillespie group which included three very familiar faces: Kenny Drew, Niels-Henning Ørsted Pedersen and Kenny Clarke, plus percussionist Humberto Canto. The band recorded ten tracks in Paris for the America label, distributed in Europe by the French company, Musidisc. The session was originally released on two LPs: *The Giant* and *The Source*. Griffin played on only two of the numbers: 'Alone Together' and 'Fiesta Mojo'. *The Giant* was digitally remastered in 2000 and released on CD by Universal in its 'Jazz in Paris' Gitanes collection.

In the autumn of 1973, Griffin was invited to join German saxophonist, Klaus Doldinger, leader of the Passport group, for a series of jubilee concerts in Germany in celebration of Doldinger's twenty-fifth anniversary as a recording artist. For these dates, the regular Passport line-up was augmented and included, in addition to Griffin, guitarists Volker Kriegel and Alexis Korner, organist Brian Auger and drummer/percussionist Pete York. The band recorded an album for Atlantic in Düsseldorf on October 13th.

Johnny Griffin and Klaus Doldinger at the Doldinger
Jubilee Concert, 1973 (photo courtesy WEA).

A couple of years later, Doldinger was to make a second
celebratory album. This time he had Les McCann, Philip
Catherine, Buddy Guy and Pete York, as well as Johnny
Griffin, guesting with the band to record the Atlantic album,
Doldinger Jubilee 1975, in Onkel Pö's Carnegie Hall in
Hamburg.

Earlier that year, on July 16th, Griffin found himself much more in his musical element when he joined Dizzy Gillespie's band for a concert at the Montreux Jazz Festival, together with his old sparring partner Lockjaw Davis, Milt Jackson, Tommy Flanagan, Niels-Henning Ørsted Pedersen and Mickey Roker. Norman Granz recorded this memorable session, *The Dizzy Gillespie Big Seven at the Montreux Jazz Festival 1975*, for his Pablo label and the eulogistic comments in Benny Green's booklet note are well merited.

Commenting on the rapport between Griffin and Davis, Green observed that, when they work together, 'the text for the day is that there are more ways than one of swinging a cat . . . Clearly, in the case of Lockjaw and Griffin, there are aspects of each player's style which strike sparks in the other, and even though they are distinctly, even profoundly, different types of saxophonists, they have two essentials in common – a magnificent instrumental command and what you might call progressive musical sensibilities . . . The two of them make an amazing pair, who bring enlightenment and great delight to all saxophone students.'

Four days after the Montreux session Johnny was in Antibes to record another album for Norman Granz' Pablo label – Roy Eldridge's *Decidedly* – which also featured Milt Jackson, plus Joe Pass, Ray Bryant, Niels-Henning Ørsted Pedersen and Louie Bellson.

In January the following year, Griffin joined the Peter Herbolzheimer All Star Big Band for a Jazz Gala concert tour, which comprised dates in Hamburg, Hannover, Düsseldorf, Frankfurt and Wiesbaden. This eighteen-piece ensemble boasted such luminaries as Ack van Rooyen, Art Farmer, Herb Geller, Wilton Gaynair, Jiggs Whigham, Slide Hampton, Albert Mangelsdorff, Volker Kriegel, Wolfgang

Dauner, Niels-Henning Ørsted Pedersen, Grady Tate, Alex Riel and Nippy Noya, plus special guests Nat Adderley, Stan Getz, Gerry Mulligan and 'Toots' Thielemans.

The Hannover concert was recorded by Atlantic and released under the title *Jazz Gala Concert*. In April 1976, Griffin made his first tour of Japan, accompanied by Horace Parlan, Mads Vinding and Arthur Taylor. The quartet recorded the album *Live in Tokyo* at the Yuhbinchokin Hall for Nippon Phonogram. Johnny was back on tour with Peter Herbolzheimer's All Star Big Band in January 1977 and the concert in the Philipshalle, Düsseldorf, was recorded by Telefunken-Decca and released on a double LP, *Jazz Gala 77*.

14

Back in the USA

In the autumn of 1978, Johnny Griffin was back in the States to guest on the Nat Adderley Galaxy album, *A Little New York Midtown Music*, recorded in Berkeley, California, on September 18th and 19th, with Victor Feldman, Ron Carter and Roy McCurdy. And, that same month, he made his first live US appearances for fifteen years when he undertook a seventeen-date tour with pianist Ronnie Mathews and bassist Ray Drummond, along with drummer Kenny Washington on some dates and Keith Copeland on others. The tour was arranged by Dexter Gordon's manager and future wife, Maxine Gregg.

'Dexter had been trying for some time to get me to come back to the States,' recalls Johnny. 'In 1974, he wanted me to come and play with him in the Apartment, a club in my home city of Chicago. But we never got it together. Then, in 1976, he came to Europe and we had this gig together in Le Havre. He told me about the great reception he had had on his return to the States.'

Maxine Gregg came to Europe in January 1978 and met Johnny at the home of Dutch promoter, Wim Wigt. They discussed the possibility of Johnny doing a US tour and decided the time was right. Griffin had been planning to return anyway to see his ex-wife, their children and his ninety-eight-year-old grandmother. So Maxine set up the tour for the autumn of 1978.

The audiences on that tour included an entirely new generation of fans and he received much the same tumultuous welcome as had been accorded two years earlier to his great friend and fellow-expatriate, Dexter Gordon. Dexter's triumphant return to his homeland, after being resident in Europe since September 1962, had been the big jazz event of 1976.

Griffin told Bill Moody in his interview for *The Jazz Exiles*:

'I had forgotten how well American audiences could react. Americans can relate to it because it's part of our own culture, yet on the whole they tend to hear things a little more superficially . . . Europeans really appreciate the music, but Americans are more spontaneous. I can feel the thirst for the music when I walk out on stage. Americans talk to the musicians while they're playing. They encourage them to play harder. And the musicians respond. It's fun playing for Americans.'

For that 1978 tour, he was extremely well served by his sidemen. Ronnie Mathews, forty-two, from Brooklyn, New York, had built an impressive reputation since leaving the Manhattan School of Music with a BA degree in 1959. Mathews took his early inspiration from Art Tatum and Bud Powell and was later strongly influenced by Thelonious Monk and Horace Silver. He had spells with Kenny Dorham, Max Roach, Freddie Hubbard, Art Blakey and Clark Terry and toured Europe and Japan with Roach and Blakey. In 1976, he joined Woody Shaw, Stafford James and Louis Hayes to accompany Dexter Gordon on his US tour.

For the next four years, Mathews was a key member of the Johnny Griffin Quartet and, in an interview with me on 18th February 2007, he spoke of this period as one of the highlights of his career:

'This was a very special group and I think Johnny regards it as one of the best bands he fronted. It was a very integrated unit and every night was an exciting experience – a lot of fun and good feeling, a lot of satisfaction and a lot of satisfied audiences. Johnny is a very special guy. He's not only a giant of a musician, but he is a good friend with a great sense of humour. He is super-energetic and lots of fun to work with.

'You've got to have fun when you're on the road – because it can be kinda gruelling, bouncing from city to city, hotel to hotel, language to language. You've got to get onstage and make everybody happy, even though you might be completely exhausted, because that's what they came there for. You can't tell them you didn't get any sleep – that's not their problem.

'Johnny Griffin is one of the unique voices in our music. He has a tremendous ability to get over the horn – he was always up-front technically. The outstanding players in jazz – such as Johnny – have not only been innovators but musicians with a very distinctive voice. As soon as you hear a sequence of notes from Griff, you know it can only be him.

'We really had some fantastic nights with Johnny. I particularly remember playing at Ronnie Scott's in London, where we would be booked for a two-week engagement. The fact that we were in the same venue for a two-week period and didn't have to worry about catching a plane at seven in the morning meant that we could be really relaxed and feel "at home" – depending, of course, on what kind of trouble we'd got into the night before!'

It was Mathews who brought the thirty-one-year-old bassist Ray Drummond into Griffin's quartet. A native of Brookline, Massachusetts, Drummond began his professional career in San Francisco with violinist Michael White and subsequently worked with Bobby Hutcherson, the Thad Jones/Mel Lewis Orchestra, George Coleman, and Slide Hampton. A powerful player with a big sound, Drummond was often compared with Paul Chambers for his time, tone and attack.

At twenty, drummer Kenny Washington, from New York, was *le Benjamin* of the quartet and a genuine revelation. He had worked with Kenny Burrell, Cedar Walton, Milt Jackson, Frank Wess and Ron Carter and he played with the kind of crisp attack and vitality that made him the ideal choice for Griffin: 'I first heard him backing Betty Carter and I was so impressed that I just had to steal him from her!'

Griffin's self-imposed European exile had kept him out of the jazz headlines in the USA for a decade and a half – even though some news did filter back about his prodigious work with the Clarke–Boland Big Band in Europe. But his return for that memorable 1978 tour emphatically sparked a major revival in the career and international acclaim of the Little Giant. The climax of the tour, after performances at the Monterey and Ann Arbor festivals, occurred on September 23rd 1978 when he joined Dexter Gordon – who had relocated to Manhattan earlier that year – and George Cables (piano), Rufus Reid (bass) and Eddie Gladden (drums) for a concert in New York's Carnegie Hall, which won a standing ovation.

An all-star group at the Jazz Showcase venue, Blackstone Hotel, Chicago, in August 1981. *Left to right*: Ronnie Mathews, Kirk Lightsey, Clifford Jordan, Griffin, Eddie Harris, Fred Anderson, Rufus Reid, Don Pate, Duane Eubanks, Ray Drummond, Marshall Thompson, Kenny Washington, Eddie Gladden (hidden) and Wilbur Campbell (photo Joe Segal).

Says Johnny, 'It was so wonderful to stand in the middle of the Carnegie Hall stage and have everyone in the audience applauding before I even played a note. It was the same at Keystone Korner in San Francisco and at the Monterey Jazz Festival. A musician can feel when the audience is friendly and positive. I want to turn the audience on to my particular experience, the highlights and the lowlights, the ups and downs. All I can do is try to stay in shape by practice and being mentally and emotionally prepared. Sometimes I feel myself stepping outside my body and watching myself play, like having nothing to do with it.

'The music's always fun, because you can play the same tune a million different ways. And when the rhythm section is swinging and the people are really feeling good – man! Oh baby, I feel guilty for feeling so good!'

Johnny said at the time that the Carnegie Hall concert was like a Hollywood ending. 'Except,' he added, 'that this is not the end – it's the beginning.'

And so it proved. After that acclaimed tour, his career enjoyed international regeneration with a series of superb albums for Galaxy and triumphant appearances at international festivals.

He told me: 'Jazz is life – so long as there is life, there will always be jazz. I'm still playing substantially what I was playing twenty years ago – and so is Dexter. That's our musical vocabulary, and we're still talking the same musical language.'

After that Carnegie Hall concert, Griffin went into the Fantasy Studios in Berkeley on October 17th to record *The Return of the Griffin* for Galaxy, with Ronnie Mathews, Ray Drummond and Keith Copeland. In his note for the album, the producer, Orrin Keepnews, wrote:

'When I learned in the fall of '78 that Johnny Griffin would be coming from Europe for his first American tour in fifteen years, I bluntly informed his manager that, no matter what, he would be recording here and I would be the producer. No other possibility was even to be considered. "That's funny," Maxine Gregg replied, "that's exactly what Griff said."'

Despite the tremendous success of that US tour, Johnny never considered returning permanently to America. But in April and May of the following years, he came back regularly to make a four-week tour of the USA, and would celebrate his birthday on April 24th with a one-week gig at Joe Segal's Jazz Showcase in his home city of Chicago.

One of the most celebrated and longest-running jazz venues in the States, the Jazz Showcase first opened its doors in 1947, when Joe Segal began presenting jazz as a Roosevelt University student. Over the years it has presented a host of major jazz artists, including Gene Ammons, Ernestine Anderson, Louie Bellson, Dee Dee Bridgewater, Ray Brown, Maynard Ferguson, Dexter Gordon, Hampton Hawes, Joe Henderson, Milt Jackson, Ahmad Jamal, Elvin Jones, Roland Kirk, Russell Malone, Junior Mance, Marian McPartland, James Moody, Pharaoh Sanders, Sonny Stitt, Sir Charles Thompson, McCoy Tyner and, on numerous occasions, Johnny Griffin.

After the Bee Hive Club closed in 1956, the Jazz Showcase became Chicago's major jazz venue, specialising in the presentation of bebop musicians. Over the next fifty years, Joe Segal presented Jazz Showcase events in scores of different locations, including the majestic Blackstone Hotel where it was based for fifteen years. The last Jazz Showcase venue was a building in the heart of Chicago at 59 West Grand Avenue, just north of Chicago's Loop and four blocks west of Michigan Avenue.

It was Segal who wrote the sleeve note for the 1958 reissue of Griffin's 1956 Argo LP, *J.G.* At this time he was Chicago correspondent for the jazz magazine, *Metronome*. He concluded his note with this observation: 'I imagine a musician of Johnny's stature, when finally he receives some public recognition, after having had years of scuffle and experience poured through his horn and whole being, must feel as though a tremendous weight has been lifted from his shoulders. Having known Johnny for many of those "nothing" years, I have the same feeling; people no longer look at me in that strange "who?" or "so-what" manner when I extol one of my very favourite tenor saxophonists . . . Finally, they have come to realise that what they've been hearing, and taking so much for granted for so many years, was, when they first heard it, a signal of things to come . . . And, by gosh, they've finally caught up to the improvising genius that is Johnny Griffin.'

Segal first met Griffin in 1947 when he was organising jam sessions at Roosevelt University. He recalls: 'Johnny had just left the Lionel Hampton band and was working with the Joe Morris Quintet. He would come up and jam with Ira Sullivan, Von Freeman, Andrew Hill, Richard Davis and many other major jazz artists.

'In 1957, I started presenting concerts all around Chicago and Johnny was a regular attraction. He played for me throughout the late 1950s at a place called the Gate of Horn. This was a folk music venue which was opened by Albert Grossman in 1956 and which presented such artists as Bob Gibson, Josh White, Odetta and Joan Baez. But on Monday nights – the off-nights – we took over with jazz, and that was really the beginning of the Jazz Showcase concept. Then, in the 1960s, I began presenting concerts at the North Park Hotel on Sunday afternoons and evenings.'

Writing about the 1960s Chicago jazz scene in the February 18th 1960 issue of *Down Beat* magazine, Gene Lees observed: 'It is on the south side that you find the most typical Chicago jazz of today. Here, a truly surprising variety of young talent is growing up. Here you will find the habitat of two of the most respected exponents and spokesmen for Chicago Jazz 1960: Johnny Griffin and Ira Sullivan.

'Big-toned and virile-sounding saxophonist Griffin has been described as one of the best of the "angry young tenors". Small of stature, affable, warm, witty and with a gift for colourful turns of speech, he seems the least likely candidate for the label "angry". Yet he does not quarrel with it. For a decade of scuffling for a recognition that has been coming to him in quantity only in the last couple of years has left him with a deeply emotional core. "I can't be a quiet player," he says. "Something is always trying to get out. I'm not suited for ballads."'

It was after Johnny's first trip back to the States since his move to Europe in 1963, that Joe Segal inaugurated what was to become an annual Jazz Showcase event. He recounts: 'I have the same birthday as Johnny – April 24th – and, every year for the next couple of decades, he would come to Chicago to play at the Showcase in a birthday celebration concert. As I recall, in 1980, we had a triple celebration at the Blackstone Hotel because Joe Henderson, who also has the same birthday, joined Johnny on that occasion.'

Griffin and Joe Segal celebrating their birthday, April 24th 2004, at Chicago's Jazz Showcase. On the left, holding the cake, is Segal's son, Wayne (photo courtesy Joe Segal).

Segal regards Griffin as one of the greatest tenor saxophonists of all time. 'I think he is better than a lot of other players, who get all the accolades. He certainly outblew Joe Henderson on that occasion and he held his own with Dexter Gordon, too. Some of my favourite recordings are those he did with Monk and with the Clarke-Boland Big Band.'

Griffin with Joe Henderson at the Jazz Showcase, Blackstone Hotel, Chicago in the 1990s (photo Joe Segal).

It was a source of genuine gratification for Griff to make those annual trips to his home country, because it gave him a chance to meet up again with his family and friends and to enjoy reunions with some of the great rhythm section masters he had worked with in the past.

Talking about his fifteen-year absence from the USA to Marc Vasey in a December 1979 interview for CKUA Radio in Edmonton, Alberta, Johnny said:

'Of course, I missed my family and friends and missed playing with the cats. I felt bad about missing my family for quite a few years. But I'm not a person who deals in nostalgia. I deal in *now*! I get my juices and positiveness out of the life forces that are happening now. Charlie Parker said *Now's the Time* and I tend to agree with him. If I'd stayed in the States, I think I would have been dead, because I was really misusing my body, drinking too much and not eating right. I had broken up with my wife and I was really depressed because things hadn't turned out the way I would have liked them to.'

Griffin also told Vasey that he felt that his native country was 'going down the drain . . . The gap between the rich and poor is greater than ever. It hurts me to walk around Chicago and see good stone buildings all gutted out. And I know why they are letting these places run down – it is because they want the residents out, to resettle them, so that they can rebuild the houses and turn them into places the less well-off people can't afford. These things hurt me. And the American people are still as politically naïve as they ever were. It is terrible when there is an election and only twenty-five per cent of the people vote. People have that apathy because they don't think their vote will change anything. It's a terrible thing to see a great country going down the drain.'

He re-asserted his preference for the European lifestyle in a December 1993 *Cadence* interview with Alwyn and Laurie Lewis: 'I'm enjoying myself so much where I am. I live in the country. I feel comfortable where I am. It's nice. I'm living in a foreign land, can't speak the language well . . . just a smattering of French. I tear the language up. You have to be born with that masculine/feminine thing. Sometimes they inter-

Recipients of the Lifetime Achievement Awards at the Jazz Showcase in Chicago, 2005. *Left to right*: Franz Jackson, Ira Sullivan, Johnny Griffin, Joe Segal, Von Freeman (photo courtesy Joe Segal).

view me on the French radio and it's hilarious. I make a lot of *faux pas* – foot-in-the-mouth disease, Griffin style.

'But, you know, I got tired of people telling me what I could and couldn't do in New York – agents and others. The whole scene was sad. For me, anyway. I went to Holland first and then I went to Paris and worked in the Blue Note for six months.

'The French taught me how to relax and got me off that New York treadmill – running, running, running – and going no place. I never felt that I had to go back to New York. I stayed in Europe for fifteen years without ever going back to the States. Not once. It's true that I missed playing with some of the fantastic musicians I had worked with over the years, and I missed seeing my family – but other than that, I had no reason to go back to the States.'

After *The Return of the Griffin*, Johnny recorded three more albums for Galaxy between October 1978 and November 1979 – *Bush Dance* with Cedar Walton (piano), George Freeman (guitar), Sam Jones (bass), Albert Heath (drums) and Kenneth Nash (percussion); *NYC Underground* with Ronnie Mathews, Ray Drummond and Idris Muhammad (drums) live at the Village Vanguard – Johnny was very insistent about recording at the Vanguard because it was his first gig at the club; and *To the Ladies*, with the same rhythm section. This last album included 'Miriam', a composition dedicated to Johnny's wife. Also included were some other originals, which could conceivably be considered as having some sexual connotation. One number is entitled 'Honey Bucket' and there is a three-part suite called 'Soft and Furry', which has sections titled 'The Entrance', 'Deep in the Middle' and 'Exit'. Johnny refers to it as his pornographic suite.

15

Europe, America
and the Avant-garde

In February 1979, Griffin played a two-week engagement at Ronnie Scott's Club and his performance throughout was a most eloquent and forceful reaffirmation of his musical integrity. As with the music, so with the man. When I interviewed him at that time for *Jazz Journal International*, of which I was then features editor, the little giant proved himself to be a direct, expressive, animated and transparently honest conversationalist.

As we talked, it was very clear that he had no time for hypocrisy and he put down people he regarded as musical pretenders in a most affably derisive way – not with malice, but with a kind of mischievous and gently mocking rationale: 'Aw, come on – *we* know he's kidding, *he* knows he's kidding, so why do the critics act like he's the new musical Messiah?'

Then he added, with that most infectious laugh: 'But I'm not calling any names. I get into trouble everywhere I go when I open my big mouth!'

About his move from the USA to Europe in 1963, he said:
'I was always able to work in the States and I appeared at Birdland pretty regularly, but I couldn't seem to get myself a

more comfortable living standard. There was no guarantee that I could do it in Europe – but I felt like giving it a try; and a man has to do what he feels like doing.

'Life in Europe has really worked out beautifully. It has been an enriching experience and, apart from one or two lean moments, there has always been plenty of work. So I resolved that, as far as going back to the States was concerned, I wasn't going to ask *them*. They had to ask *me*. Everything had to be set up right – that's why I waited. I wasn't in any hurry because life in Europe was beautiful. I certainly wasn't going to sneak back into the States with nobody knowing I'd been and gone!

'Dexter really set the pace. He was a giant when I was still in high school but it took America more than thirty years to discover him. Dexter went back in 1976 and really tore the place apart. I went over in the wake of all that goodwill.

'I had forgotten what American audiences are like. But, of course, they really respond to jazz. It's their music, after all. I couldn't even finish my solos before people were on their feet applauding. It was fantastic.

'It was really overwhelming – and it made me wonder where all those beautiful people had been when I was living there and scuffling!'

Johnny told me that, while he was delighted to see so many of his contemporaries working and still playing 'the real music', he was dismayed by the proliferation of jazz-rock and disco-jazz in the States. He said, 'Once again, I don't want to call any names – but the music is so *sad*. It has nothing to do with jazz. Well, let me qualify that – it has nothing to do with the music *I'm* into and I've always thought of what I do as jazz. I've come to the conclusion that jazz is not for the masses but just for those people who are able to perceive it and look through the surface of the music to what is inside.

'You get all this talk about avant-garde music, but who plays it, apart from guys in a few lofts in New York and one or two guys in Europe? I can't imagine them going into Harlem and playing that stuff. They'd get lynched . . .'

And, as he warmed to this subject, Griffin became a little casual about his embargo on name-calling:

'I know there are some very good musicians involved in the avant-garde movement. And I like a lot of the guys personally. But I cannot dig their music. In December 1967, Archie Shepp's group came to play in Le Chat Qui Pêche. I went down to the club because I wanted to listen to these cats play. I remembered that in October of that year, when I played in Stockholm with Monk, the Shepp band was also on that same George Wein tour.

'I was in my hotel room [during that tour] getting ready for the evening, when the telephone rang. It was Archie Shepp and he wanted to see me. I told him to come to the room and I gave him a cognac and a little puffy-wuffy. "Archie," I said to him, "why are you making all that noise with your saxophone? You are doing everything that I was taught not to do and what I wouldn't want to do." And he told me, very sincerely, that that was the way American society made him feel. And that shut my mouth – bam! – because I was in exile myself, in a way of speaking.

'So when I went down to the Chat Qui Pêche a couple of months later, I wanted to make sure that I heard this group with open ears. And there, sitting in the audience was New Orleans clarinettist Albert Nicholas. The Shepp group started playing and they sounded just as disturbing then as they did when I heard them in Stockholm or on record. Albert, the grand old man, looked at me and said, "Johnny, what are they doing?" And I said, "Albert, I have no idea."

'I went back two nights later to make sure, and Albert was sitting right there. This time, when the Shepp group started playing, he said, "I know what they're doing." And I answered, "Then can you please tell me?" But Albert said he couldn't explain. And later, Dexter went down to the club to play with them. I thought I must be going tone deaf. Dexter only played for a few minutes with the group, then split. Were Albert and Dexter afraid they might be missing something?

'I remember Don Byas once told Archie Shepp that he couldn't play. I didn't think anybody in that band could play. Shepp had Grachan Moncur III and Roswell Rudd on trombone, Jimmy Garrison on bass and Beaver Harris on drums. Jimmy Garrison kept crying for John Coltrane and Shepp kept telling him, "This is not John Coltrane's band, this is Archie Shepp's."

'Then there's Ornette Coleman. How can people take his trumpet and violin playing seriously? Come on, that's just ridiculous. Music is supposed to be beautiful. Music *is* beauty. It shouldn't sound like a bad LSD trip – what's wrong with having a beautiful sound on your instrument? OK, you can still play rough and aggressive, as long as it's making some musical sense and swinging. But some of that avant-garde stuff is a negation of music. Listen, if cats like that had got up on the bandstand in New York twenty-five years ago, the rhythm section would have walked off and they'd have been left up there by themselves.

'A lot of these cats just can't play. And others can play, but can't swing. Take Cecil Taylor. The cat cannot swing. Duke Ellington said it: "It don't mean a thing . . ." You know the rest. OK, so that marks me down as a small-minded, fossilized musical thinker. But how can jazz all of a sudden go completely crazy and have no form?

'There was no jazz before this avant-garde mess that didn't swing. All the music, from spirituals, to gospel, to the blues – all of it had swing in common. Look, I can go up on stage and make as much noise as any avant-garde player, but I dare any of them to come up and swing.'

For all his disparagement of so-called new directions in jazz, Johnny said he had no fears about the future of the music.

'Jazz is life,' he told me.

'So long as there is life, there will always be jazz. There have always been critics who have been trying to kill jazz for as long as I can remember. But I'm still here and the cats like Dexter and Frank Foster and George Coleman are still here, blowing and swinging. And, as long as guys swing, jazz cannot die.

'I'm still playing substantially what I was playing twenty years ago, and so is Dexter – but that's our musical vocabulary, and we're still talking the same musical language. I guess our playing has matured over the years, and certainly cats have found new ways of playing bass and drums, but fundamentally it's the same music. If you listen to a solo that Lester Young played in the thirties, the arrangement sounds dated and the rhythm section sounds dated, but what Prez plays sounds just as good and fresh now as it did then. Real jazz, real music, survives.'

For his American tour and for his stint at the Scott Club, Griffin used an all-American rhythm section, which was something of a luxury because he had had to adjust to playing with Europeans most of his time in Europe. And, despite the great progress made by jazz musicians in Europe since Griff first settled on the Continent, an adjustment, he said in 1979, was still necessary.

'Then again, I know plenty of black Americans from the ghettoes who can't play jazz, can't swing, can't even keep time. No sense of rhythm at all. But I guess if you do have a musical gift, then New York is the best place to develop it. The atmosphere can really be stimulating. But the gap between American and European musicians really has narrowed tremendously.'

The respect that European musicians have for the musicianship of the leading American jazzmen was one of the factors that originally induced Johnny Griffin to make his home in Europe. When I interviewed him for the first time in 1965, he had described the conditions of life in the United States as 'deplorable' and said that the real problem was that jazz musicians were not given credit for having any dignity.

In 1979 he was able to comment that: 'Musicians got angry with the public because they didn't get the respect they deserved; there were tremendous social pressures – for white people as well as blacks; and clubs were closing down. Everyone was pessimistic and I suppose one product of that depressing period was the emergence of avant-garde extremists with all that anger and agony in their music. Now, though, conditions seem to have improved a great deal – and maybe this has something to do with the return of real music. Swinging music.'

16

Chateau Bellevue

It is an incontrovertible fact that you can count the number of jazz musicians from the South Side of Chicago, who now live in a beautiful, ten-room, nineteenth century chateau in France, on the thumb of one hand. And that one musician is the Little Giant, Johnny Griffin.

In the spring of 1980, Johnny and his wife left Bergambacht and moved back to France, having decided that they preferred a warmer climate. They set up home in an apartment near Cimiez on the Côte d'Azur, the location of the annual Nice Jazz Festival. But they really wanted a house with a garden and, after nine months in Cimiez, they found their desirable residence in Roquefort-les-Bains, a town about ten miles to the east of Cannes, where they stayed for the next three years.

In April 1980, Johnny joined Monty Alexander, Ray Brown and Martin Drew at the Tonstudio Bauer in Ludwigsburg to record the double LP, *Summerwind*, for the German Jeton label. The quartet actually recorded seventeen titles, of which fourteen were released on the double LP. In 1998 a different selection was put together for a fifteen-track

CD released by Kingston World. In the booklet, Werner Stiefele notes that the recording engineer, Carlos Albrecht, made a double recording of the session – one direct to disc and one on a digital two-track tape.

In June 1981, Griffin saluted his old friend, Babs Gonzales, with the composition, 'Blues For Gonzi', when he appeared with Ronnie Mathews, Ray Drummond and Kenny Washington at the Village Vanguard. This title, along with 'A Monk's Dream' and '56', a Griff original on the chords of the Herb Magidson/Allie Wrubel tune, 'The Masquerade Is Over', is featured on two Jazz Legends DVDs produced by Ben Sidran.

One of the DVDs, *Art Blakey and the Jazz Messengers: Live at the Village Vanguard Club*, has three additional tracks by Art Blakey's Jazz Messengers, also recorded at the Vanguard, with Wynton Marsalis, Branford Marsalis, Billy Pierce, Donald Brown and Charles Fambrough. The other DVD, *Jazz Life*

Johnny and Miriam Griffin's chateau in France (photo David Redfern).

The Little Giant sits in front of his big chateau (photo David Redfern).

Volume 1, has five additional tracks by the quintet of tenor saxophonist Richie Cole.

Recalling the DVD project in his book *A Life in the Music*, Ben Sidran wrote:

'In June, we taped the first four programmes for the *Jazz Life* Pioneer Laserdisc series . . . We had the best cameramen in New York City and Stan Dorfman, a pioneer in music television, directing. I had negotiated with Max Gordon, the owner of the Village Vanguard, to use his club, and had arranged with Johnny Griffin, Nat Adderley, Art Blakey and Chico Hamilton to be participants. We were shooting two shows a day for two days, and by nine o'clock on the morning of the first shoot, we had three huge trucks lined up outside the club on Seventh Avenue, with huge cable snakes running everywhere. Guys were carrying lights and cameras down the narrow stairs and into the dim recesses of this jazz institution.

'Max Gordon, who was already well into his seventies and had been running the place for forty years, sat in the kitchen smoking his cigars, nonplussed, watching the action.'[10]
He described meeting Griffin coming down the stairs. 'He had a wide smile on his face. I told him I was happy to see him, and he said, "I bet you are." His band set up quickly and by 3 p.m. the invited audience filed in and we were taping, right on schedule. After the opening number, Johnny stepped up to the microphone and said, "Jazz music! Your music! Our music!" The crowd applauded madly, lovingly, happy to be in the presence of a healer, and Johnny said, "This music is made by and for people who have chosen to feel good in spite of conditions," and I started clapping and screaming along with the rest.'

On July 11th 1983, Johnny was in the Rudy Van Gelder studio in Englewood Cliffs, New Jersey, with an all-star group assembled by his old colleague, Philly Joe Jones, to pay tribute to the great composer, arranger and pianist, Tadley Ewing 'Tadd' Dameron. With trumpeter Don Sickler as musical director, the album, *Look Stop Listen*, on the Uptown label, featured Philly Joe, Virgil Jones, Benny Powell, Frank Wess, Johnny Griffin, Charles Davis, Cecil Payne, Walter Davis Jr. and Larry Ridley. A couple of weeks later, Griffin was back in the Fantasy Studios in Berkeley, California, to record another album for Galaxy – *Call it Whachawana* – with his new quartet: Mulgrew Miller on piano, Curtis Lundy on bass and Kenny Washington on drums – all three, as Orrin Keepnews observed in the liner notes, 'graduates of a valuable jazz school named Betty Carter.' This was Johnny's twentieth album for Keepnews.

Griffin's original twelve-bar theme, 'Call it Whachawana', also featured on the album *Keep on Comin'*, which Jimmy

Smith recorded with Johnny, Kenny Burrell and Mike Baker for the Elektra/Musician label on September 3rd 1983 at the Atlanta Free Jazz Festival. In his note for the album, Smith recalls that he and Griffin had played together thirty years earlier, when Jimmy sat in on piano with Johnny's group. He notes that, after he played his solo piano medley at the Atlanta Festival, Griff said to him, 'You've been practising!'

Johnny and Miriam stayed in Roquefort-les-Pins for three years and then, on February 4th 1984, they moved to the Chateau Bellevue, which is located in Availles Limousine in the Vienne *département* of France, between Poitiers and Limoges and about 250 miles from Paris. Built in 1810, the ten-room chateau stands in fifteen hectares (thirty-seven acres) of land.

Recalling the move, Johnny told me: 'We discovered the property through a friend of ours – Francis Paudras – who lived in the area. It had lain uninhabited for five years, so it needed quite a lot of work to restore it. We are very happy here. It is so peaceful and in such a beautiful area – a farming region right on top of the cognac district, which I suppose makes it an appropriate location for me! I understand that about twenty people lived here previously, but some of the young men gambled all the money away and they had to sell parts of the estate to pay their debts.'

In the summer of 1984 I had the idea of assembling a band of American musicians who were resident in Paris during the city's 'golden age' of jazz. I discussed the idea with Kenny Clarke, the spiritual leader of the jazz expatriates, and he was enthusiastic. I also talked about the project with Nathan Davis. His reaction, too, was very positive. The plan was to assemble an eight-piece band to tour the European festival circuit in the summer of 1985. As Klook was seventy years old, it was decided that drumming duties would be shared between him and another drummer, as in the Clarke–Boland Big Band. Billy Brooks, based in Berne, Switzerland, was signed up to be the second drummer. The other founder members, in addition to Griffin and Davis, were Woody Shaw and Dizzy Reece (trumpets), Slide Hampton (trombone), Kenny Drew (piano) and Jimmy Woode (bass).

Ina Dittke, a young New York-based booking agent from Düsseldorf, took on the job of setting up the Paris Reunion Band's first European tour. But, sadly, Kenny Clarke, the man for whom the band was created, never got to play with his

The Paris Reunion Band, Tring, 1985: *standing, left to right:* booking agent Ina Dittke, Johnny Griffin, Kenny Drew, Nathan Davis, Jimmy Woode, Woody Shaw, Dizzy Reece, Mike Hennessey; *squatting at front:* Slide Hampton; (photo David Redfern).

former Paris colleagues. In the early hours of January 26th 1985, he suffered a fatal heart attack. The funeral, in Montreuil-sous-Bois on January 29th, was attended by Johnny Griffin, along with Hal Singer, Steve Lacy, Bobby Few, Jimmy Gourley, Nancy Holloway, Lou Bennett, Herbie Hancock and Manu Dibango, among many others.

The Paris Reunion Band made its inaugural tour in June and July 1985, playing concerts at the North Sea Jazz Festival in The Hague, Montreux, Antibes, San Sebastian, Berlin, Paris, Athens and Tring in the UK. It recorded its début album, *French Cooking*, for Sonet on July 3rd 1985 and went on to record three more Sonet albums and one for the German label, Amiga. But Griffin's spell with the band was short-lived. It was not long before his preference for working with small ensembles reasserted itself. He left after that first tour and was succeeded by Joe Henderson.

The PRB played dates in Europe and the United States over the next four years, but when Woody Shaw died on May 10th 1989, Nathan Davis decided to disband the group. He said, 'The death of Woody kind of killed the Paris Reunion Band, for me anyway. I mean, we did some concerts after that, but it sort of petered out.'

Speaking of Johnny Griffin's early departure from the PRB, Davis said, 'Of course, Johnny was always happiest when he was working with just a rhythm section. But he joined the PRB as a gesture to me and out of his respect for Klook.'

However, for his recordings over the next decade, Griffin departed from his customary quartet line-up and made albums with a variety of combos.

On September 7th and 8th 1986, he joined Benny Bailey, Horace Parlan, Hein van de Geyn and Ed Thigpen in the

Daylight Recording Studio in Brussels to record the Deborah Brown album, *Euroboppin'*, for Alfa Jazz.

In October 1987 he was in Barcelona with Ben Sidran, Jimmy Woode, Ben Riley and French singer Clementine to make the Orange Blue album, *Have You Met . . . Barcelona?* And, in December of that year, for the same label, he recorded *Continent Bleu* in Paris, with Clementine, Patrice Galas on keyboards, Niels-Henning Ørsted Pedersen, Bobby Durham and percussionist Freddy Citadelle.

It was back to the tried and tested quartet format in May the following year for the album *Take My Hand*, which featured Johnny with Michael Weiss (piano), Dennis Irwin (bass) and Kenny Washington (drums). The session was recorded at the Studio in the Grove in Davie, Florida, by the RTV Communications Group Inc. and licensed to ARC

Take My Hand, recorded in May 1988.

Music. The booklet was written by Orrin Keepnews' son, Peter, and the cover picture of the Little Giant on the sleeve was taken by Miriam Griffin.

*   *   *

In June 1989, French promoter Jean-François Deiber, organizer of the annual TBB (Théâtre Boulogne-Billancourt) jazz festival, decided to pay tribute to Charlie Parker and booked an all-star septet, led by trumpeter/arranger Don Sickler, to perform at the festival. Three members of the group – baritone saxophonist Cecil Payne, pianist Duke Jordan and drummer Roy Haynes – were former Parker sidemen and they were joined by Johnny Griffin, as well as Jackie McLean on alto saxophone and Ron Carter on bass. The session, which featured ten great Parker classics – 'Yardbird Suite', 'Parkers Mood', 'Chasin' the Bird', 'Big Foot', 'Donna Lee', 'Shaw 'Nuff', 'Billie's Bounce', 'Relaxin' at Camarillo', 'Scrapple from the Apple' and 'Dewey Square' – plus a Don Sickler original, 'Bird Lives', and the standard, 'Don't Blame Me', was recorded for the Verve label and released in two volumes under the title, *Birdology*.

In October 1990, Johnny was in New York with another all-star group to record *The Cat*, an album featuring nine Griffin compositions arranged by pianist Michael Weiss. Lining up with Griffin were Curtis Fuller (trombone), Steve Nelson (vibes), Michael Weiss (piano), Dennis Irwin (bass) and Kenny Washington (drums). The album was released on Island Records' Antilles label, with notes by Count Basie alumnus, Frank Foster, who wrote:

'In my mind, the name Johnny Griffin automatically conjures up several prized memories of events that took place on Chicago's South Side during the early to mid-1950s. These were my initial years with the Basie Orchestra and Chicago was one of the more frequent stop-overs in our schedule at that time.

'The events referred to were mostly jam sessions in which the participants were usually various members of the Basie band and local musicians from the Chicago area. There were generally several horn players, including Griff and myself and some very good rhythm sections. But, of all the participants in those sessions, the one name I can recall besides my own is that of Johnny Griffin. This, without a doubt, is owing to the fact that in each of those sessions, I was the recipient of a "free lesson" in the art of saxophone playing from none other than "Little Chicago Fire", as I sometimes refer to Griff. I'll forever hold dear the memories of those revealing jam sessions at such places as the Swingland Café, the Bee Hive and McKie's Lounge – all South Side locations and all principal venues for jazz presentation during those eventful 1950s.

'My first ever viewing and hearing of Johnny Griffin in person was back in the mid-1940s, when he was quite a little fellow sitting in Lionel Hampton's saxophone section. I was amazed at how such a big, fat sound could come from someone not much larger than the saxophone he was playing. I wasn't even certain that his feet reached all the way to the floor as he sat. In addition, he was made to look all the more diminutive by the ample girth of the other tenor player with the band, the late, great Arnett Cobb. Never did I suspect that this little "monster" of a musician was to blow me completely away a decade later!

'His blazing speed in producing one dynamite phrase after another in rapid-fire succession seemed to be equalled only by the logic in his musical statements – not just a "lot of notes" with most of them meaning nothing – they made lots

Griffin composing at his home in France, 2007 (photo David Redfern).

of sense, told a story, were completely harmonically relevant and yet uniquely constructed in his own style.

'This recording displays a mellowed, much-matured Griff, still capable of the rapid-fire passages, but making far less use of them and more of just plain old soulful playing with every bit of that aforementioned logic, harmonic relevance, authority and originality of approach still very much in evidence. Right here in the presentation is yet another series of lessons in the art of saxophone playing, but with the added ingredient of advanced maturity. There are some pretty good lessons in composition, too.'

* * *

Griffin's compositional prowess was very much in evidence on the April 1992 Antilles album, *Dance of Passion*, which featured seven of his originals plus Cole Porter's 'All Through the Night'. Johnny was backed by a six-piece combo consisting of Dave Bargeron on tuba, John Clark on French horn, Steve Turre on trombone, Michael Weiss on piano, Peter Washington on bass and Kenny Washington on drums. Weiss, who had been Johnny's first-call pianist in the States since 1987, wrote the horn arrangements.

In his note for the album, Ira Gitler recalled that on his visits to the Village Vanguard or Birdland when Johnny Griffin was appearing, he would go intending to catch one set and wind up staying until the last note was sounded. 'Griff is a compelling player. He draws you into his orbit and takes you along for the ride, pushing your adrenalin button and soothing you at alternate times with his combination of soul and intellect.'

And Gitler quotes Michael Weiss as saying of Johnny:

'Two lasting things have the greatest impact. One side is his youthfulness, his *joie de vivre*, uninhibitedness, go-for-broke attitude – he loves it when you don't play it safe, even if it becomes a mistake – his irrepressible energy. The other side is that, underneath, there is an extreme concentration, a total absorption. As spontaneous as he is, he is totally immersed all the time – right on it. Inspiration comes to me from having to follow him every night.'

In late 1993, Johnny Griffin suffered the first in a debilitating succession of ailments and disorders, which, but for the devotion and determination of his wife, Miriam, would certainly have cost him his life. She recalls:

'I noticed that he got tired very quickly and had a hard time just walking around the house or opening the window shutters. So we went to a doctor in Poitiers, who told Johnny to give up playing the saxophone, get some books to read and watch television – and you can imagine how well that went down with my husband!'

Griff takes up the story:

'Fortunately, Professor Rogier Luccioni, head of the cardiology unit at the University of Marseilles (and also a bassist, by the way), heard about my problems and told me to come to the hospital without delay.'

Johnny and Miriam Griffin in the grounds of Chateau Bellevue, 2007 (photo David Redfern).

Johnny was diagnosed with blocked arteries and, in the process of their examination, it was discovered that he had had a heart attack some time earlier. The doctors carried out an angioplasty operation, which involves the use of a catheter to open the arteries. However, the angioplasty was not successful, so Johnny had to return to the hospital several months later for a further operation.

In 1999, he was hospitalized in Marseilles once again, this time with respiratory problems.

Says Miriam, 'It was discovered that he had liquid behind the lungs and the doctor told me that if I had not brought him to the hospital, he would have died. They also checked his arteries once more and had to do a further angioplasty operation. Johnny was in the hospital for two weeks.'

In an interview I had with Griffin at the Chateau Bellevue in June 2005, he repeated to me what he has often said – that moving to France from the United States in 1963 saved his life. 'The health care in France is superb,' he said. 'You get excellent treatment at a reasonable cost.'

*   *   *

On December 28th 1993, he joined the Roy Hargrove Quartet at the Mancinelli theatre in Orvieto, Italy, to record his ballad, 'When We Were One' and the Cyrus Chestnut original, 'Greens at the Chicken Shack', for the Verve album *Roy Hargrove with the 'Tenors of Our Time'*, which also featured guest appearances by Joe Henderson, Branford Marsalis, Joshua Redman and Stanley Turrentine.

Hargrove returned the compliment in December the following year, when he guested on three tracks of Johnny's album, *Chicago, New York, Paris*, which was released on the Verve label in April 1995 in celebration of Griff's fiftieth year as a professional jazz musician. Backed by Kenny Barron or

Peter Martin (piano), Rodney Whittaker or Christian McBride (bass) and Gregory Hutchinson or Victor Lewis (drums), Johnny produced inspired renditions of five of his compositions – 'The JAMFs Are Coming', 'Do It', 'To Love', 'Leave Me' and 'Not Yet', plus Michel Legrand's 'You Must Believe in Spring', Rodgers & Hart's 'My Romance', Vincent Youmans' 'Without a Song' and the traditional theme, 'Hush-a-Bye'.

In the summer of 1999, Griffin teamed up with the highly accomplished and immensely versatile pianist, Martial Solal, to record a truly outstanding duo album – *In and Out* – for Disques Dreyfus. This recording, which took place in the Studio Damiens in Boulogne-Billancourt on June 29th and 30th and July 1st, 1999, brought together two *virtuosi*, both masters of their respective instruments, and was a wonderfully creative meeting of two great musical minds. Although both men had been active on the Paris jazz scene for many years, they had only played together two or three times before this session – as Pascal Anquetil observes in the booklet. Noting that the duo formation in jazz represents a great challenge, he writes, 'It is an extremely demanding format that won't abide the slightest lapse of attention . . . What's at stake is the whole fragile art of conversation, with no safety net, no sleight of hand and no escape hatch. You have to know how to leave your ego at the door and listen – generously and receptively – to your partner.'

The album features three originals by Griffin ('Come with Me', 'Hey Now' and 'When You're in my Arms') and three by Solal ('In and Out', 'L'Oreille Est Hardie' and 'Neutralisme'), plus the standard 'You Stepped out of a Dream' and Thelonious Monk's 'Well You Needn't'.

Griffin with pianist Tommy Flanagan (*left*), gospel singer singer Vera Love and trumpet/flugelhorn player Art Farmer, in the Vienna Concert House, November 1998, for a belated celebration of Farmer's 70th birthday.

A few months later, in February 2000, Johnny recorded a second duo album – this time with pianist Horace Parlan. *Close Your Eyes*, on the Minor Music label. This was a project that label chief Stephan Meyner had had in mind for a considerable time. Recorded at Gaga Studios in Hamburg, the album features six standards, plus Monk's 'Pannonica' and Johnny's highly durable blues, 'The JAMFs Are Coming'.

In the CD booklet, Stephan Meyner observed that, in his view, Griffin never got the recognition by the public and the critics that he deserved. He added, 'You might have your own special tenor favourite, but the history of the instrument would have been another one without Griff.'

Touché!

17

Six Decades of Swinging

Johnny Griffin's illustrious career as a pre-eminent jazz musician has been characterised by his total dedication to – and unquenchable enthusiasm for – his craft. He told French writer Pierre Lattes of *Jazz Magazine* in June 1963:

'I'm in jazz because I love it. So far it has been my life's work. I imagine that, for me, it is a release from nervous tension – world affairs, confusion. It permits me to tell the world how I feel. Every time I play it's different. It's a new experience. I have had the opportunity to meet some very nice people, sympathetic to jazz. They get something out of it and it makes them feel good. And besides, it's all I want to do. I would not have chosen any other profession.'

When I interviewed Johnny in June 2006, he talked freely about his approach to jazz and offered a perceptive appraisal of the current jazz scene:

'People are saying jazz is dying and that there are no great stars any more, only imitators. They claim that nothing is happening – the future is limited and, sooner or later, jazz is going to disappear altogether.

Johnny Griffin
at home,
March 2007
(photo David
Redfern).

'I think that statement is very short-sighted – anybody
who makes a remark like that has no idea of what jazz is in
the first place. They don't have any connection with the creative forces, which are part of living life – because jazz is a
thing which changes from day to day; it shouldn't be pinned
down like they pin down rap, hip-hop and acid jazz.

'Jazz is about living life and with the many individuals we
have on this planet, there can be just as many interpretations
of what constitutes jazz. But, for me, one thing is certain – if
it doesn't swing, it's not jazz. I have never known any serious
jazz musician who did not consider swinging a vital element
in his or her playing. If you don't have African polyrhythms
in the music, it is not jazz.

'You can play your bass drum beats and your rock rhythms, your Beatles and Rolling Stones music and what have you, but this is superficial stuff. I know that people need this music and I wouldn't take it away from them. But jazz goes deep; it goes down into the music, below the surface, into the heart and soul of what's happening. Jazz is something that touches the soul, the essence of movement – to swing, to glide, to float with the life stream. That is the difference – people who say jazz is dead and can't last much longer just don't understand this.

'Then people say that the future of jazz is threatened because there are no giants any more. Others say that jazz has to move forward to survive. But for me, the music doesn't have to go forward – it's there already. It is a fundamental point that, when people evaluate classical music, they may say that there has been nothing new since Bach or Beethoven – and nobody wants to change their great music; but with jazz, people keep talking about progressing. Why must there always be change? They are not prepared to rest on what great jazz creators have done – such as Parker, Lester and Armstrong. Why can't this be the classical music of the jazz segment of the musical spectrum? Why must everything change? What is wrong with playing *Billie's Bounce* twenty years from now?

'The people who make these statements are trying to view jazz in same way as they view classical music – and I love classical music. But classical musicians don't swing. A classical musician would break his neck if he tried to swing – although he would really love it if he could. Yehudi Menuhin found that out when he played with Stéphane Grappelli.

'When I play for audiences, I try to take them into our world. I try to get them to escape from where they have been, because they are already bored. We try to take them out of their boredom by giving them some swing – something they can feel within themselves. That is the meaning of jazz. It is not where its going – jazz is already there and people ought to follow. It is so wrong when people say, "Oh, we heard that before." Because when you think about it, they heard Bach before and Beethoven before. But it is still great music – and so is the music of Armstrong and Ellington.

'Those people are listening to notes – they were never taught how to feel, they are lacking in sensitivity. That is why I say they can't discern anything below the surface of what's happening. They can't delve down into the inner core of this art form – well, it is more than an art form, it's life, it's living and it doesn't have to go any place. It is already there. That is what is so stupid. How will jazz evolve next? Evolution for what? This is life – all you need is a good feeling and a sense of fun – or "phun" as Babs Gonzales put it.

'I have been playing the same kind of swinging music all my life – and I'm delivering the same musical message today – because I am the same person. The main thing for me is to feel good and to have the people around me pick up that same emotion and to feel as good as I'm feeling, if that is possible. I realize it is not easy for them, but with the love in my heart, the support of the musicians I am playing with and that strong swing of polyrhythms from Africa, it is possible for audiences to join this feel-good happening.

'People who ask where jazz is going are completely missing the point. They should ask themselves where *they* are going. And the answer is: nowhere fast. They're running backwards.

'And you don't have to be a giant to play jazz. The midgets can do it. You don't have to have a Napoleon of jazz or a John Coltrane. Jazz doesn't have to have a reason – it's the feeling

of joy, the *joie de vivre*. The so-called jazz critics, who are har-
bingers of doom, just don't understand what jazz is all about.
Most of them can't swing anyway, even if they were hanging
by a rope from a pine tree.'

* * *

Johnny Griffin is an unremitting purist when it comes to his
approach to jazz. He has indicated on many occasions that
he has little time for the avant-garde movement and he
believes that jazz and electronics are largely incompatible. As
he said in an interview on Buffalo's National Public Radio
Station, WBFO:

'I have no respect at all for that that avant-garde stuff.
Zero.

'I once had to play a festival in a place called Tabarka
in Tunisia. Miles Davis had played there the day before. This
is a village near the Tunisian-Algerian border and we had to
take taxicabs across the desert to get there. When we
arrived, the organizers told us that when Miles went on and
plugged in his instrument, they turned on the electricity for
all his electronic stuff and all the lights in the village went
out. That's ridiculous!

'I love Ornette Coleman's compositions, which make a lot
of sense. But once he starts playing his solos – I'm finished. I
like Shostakovich, I like atonal music. But those avant-garde
jazz musicians, I don't think they are musicians – and I'm not
talking about Ornette Coleman – he is a good musician.
Anthony Braxton? Zero. So boring.

'These guys were promoted as being geniuses – another
reason why I left America. Leonard Bernstein, I think, said
that Ornette Coleman was a natural extension of Charlie
Parker. That is the dumbest, most asinine thing I ever heard.
And John Lewis agreed with him.

'When people hear these remarks, they respect the men who made them – so they think it is gospel truth and they go and see these musicians. Then they say, "Well if that's jazz, I don't like it." And that's what killed the music here in the USA in the 1960s. It doesn't swing. Nothing is happening. Jazz always had a swing, whether dixieland or straight ahead or swing or bebop. It always swung. That avant-garde music doesn't have swing. It's cacophony. Nothing.'

* * *

The label 'fastest gun in the west' has stuck to Griffin since his first Blue Note recordings in the 1950s. He referred to his mercurial technique in his interview with Art Taylor in 1969: 'I'm always talking about using my horn like a machine gun, but not to kill anybody. I want to shoot them with notes of love.' But, later, he said, 'I use a lot more space in my playing than when I was twenty-five or thirty years old. Before, I felt like I was in a rush to play everything possible – I got angry when I had to take a breath. I wanted to keep going all the time. No space – fill it up! I was always motivated to play hard. I got so excited when I played, and I still do. I want to eat up the music, just like a child eating candy. The difference is that today I can back off and control myself.'

But Griffin's playing has always had a tender side to it. You can hear this very clearly when you listen to his interpretations of Rodgers and Hart's 'My Romance' and Michel Legrand's 'You Must Believe in Spring' on the December 1994 Verve album, *Chicago–New York–Paris*: the album which celebrated Johnny's fifty years as a professional musician. His playing on these standards speaks to his sensitivity, compassion, and deep feeling for the music. And these are just two examples of many, many recorded ballads, which testify eloquently to the tender side of the Little Giant.

Johnny plays sustained notes with a Websterian vibrato. He has always had a great admiration for Ben Webster and he says, 'Ben was a real storyteller. He learned his music from Mister Willis Handy Young – Lester's father – when he was staying at their house. And that's when Prez used to take him on his gigs. He also liked the way Ben comped on the piano. It was fantastic to have been around masters like Ben, Lester, Don Byas, Lucky Thompson and Coleman Hawkins. They were really my heroes.'

'Sometimes,' says Johnny, 'when the rhythm section is really cooking and everybody is together, this feeling of euphoria comes over you. Sometimes I have to stop and laugh and I say, "My God – and I'm getting paid for this, too!"'

In a December 1979 interview with Marc Vasey on CKUA Radio Educational in Edmonton, Alberta, he said, 'Music has always been a twenty-four-hour thing with me. It is the only constant that I have ever known in my life. The love of music has sustained me.'

He has never forgotten what he considers to be his great good fortune in having been a pupil of Walter Henri Dyett. 'That was a genuine privilege for me,' he told me, 'because he really helped me to realize my potential as a musician.'

When he was on tour in the USA in 1999, Johnny was interviewed by Bob Bernotas. Looking back on his life in jazz, he said:

'This country has changed so much. When I grew up we had music appreciation classes for eight- and nine-year-old kids. We had to listen to an hour of classical music every week. But it's no more. I went back to DuSable High School where I learned music. They were honouring my late bandmaster, Walter Dyett, and I had one wish – to see once again

Busking at Bellevue – Mike Hennessey (piano) with Johnny Griffin in March, 2007 (photo David Redfern).

the band room where I had studied. But there was no band room. There was no music department. They'd cut it out!

'And I can't tell you how many kids that programme saved, kept off the streets. It kept the kids busy doing something worthwhile. Why is it they always cut music out when they have budgetary problems, like it's not necessary? They don't realize the importance of music for the emotional health of people. They're so busy commercialising everything. I think that every kid should be able to play an instrument, even if it only lasts one or two years. It brings a sensitivity to the soul that will be missing later on if it is not offered.'[II]

Johnny Griffin's Jazz Showcase lifetime achievement plaque (2005) 'for his continued dedication to providing exciting saxophone improvisation to music lovers worldwide' (photo David Redfern).

Notes

1. From the song 'My Kind of Town', words by Sammy Cahn and music by James van Heusen. Copyright © 1964 Cahn Music Co., WB Music Corp and Van Heusen Music Corp. Copyright renewed. All rights for Cahn Music Co. administered by WB Music Corp. International copyright secured. All rights reserved.

2 James Lincoln Collier, *The Making of Jazz*, London: HarperCollins, 1978.

3. The list of notable jazz musicians born in Chicago includes: Albert Ammons, Gene Ammons, Israel Crosby, Richard Davis, Dorothy Donegan, Bud Freeman, Russ Freeman, Benny Goodman, Bennie Green, Johnny Griffin, Eddie Harris, Ina Ray Hutton, Jo Jones, Quincy Jones, Clifford Jordan, Lee Konitz, Gene Krupa, Lou Levy, Meade Lux Lewis, Abbey Lincoln, Joe Marsala, Marty Marsala, Al McKibbon, Jimmy McPartland, Mezz Mezzrow, Ray Nance, Anita O'Day, Julian Priester, Bill Russo, Muggsy Spanier, Joe Sullivan, Ed Thigpen, Mel Tormé, Cy Touff, Lennie Tristano, Wilbur Ware and Jimmy Yancey.

4. In his December 1969 interview for Arthur Taylor, *Notes and Tones*, London: Quartet Books, 1987.

5. Leslie Gourse, *Straight No Chaser: The Life and Genius of Thelonious Monk*, New York: Schirmer Books, 1997.

6. *The Huckleberry Hound Show* was William Hanna and Joseph Barbera's second made-for-television series. Premiered in 1958, it starred a dim-witted, good-natured hound dog with a Southern drawl and became hugely popular.

7. Radio programme produced by Ben Sidran and broadcast on National Public Radio in the USA in March 1998.

8. Mike Hennessey, *Klook: The Story of Kenny Clarke*, London: Quartet, 1990.

9. Bill Moody, *The Jazz Exiles*, Reno: University of Nevada Press, 1993.

10. Ben Sidran, *A Life in the Music*, Lanham, Maryland: Taylor Trade Publishing, 2003.

12. Bob Bernotas, 1994 interview with Johnny Griffin, revised 1999: *www.melmartin.com* (last visited February 2008).

Saxophone straps (photo David Redfern).

Albums

(Johnny Griffin as leader or co-leader)

Johnny Griffin with the Joe Morris Orchestra: New York, 1946–1949. Classics 5057

Little Johnny Griffin and his Orchestra: Chicago, c. April 1953. Okeh 7036

J. G.: Johnny Griffin Quartet: Chicago, c. 1956. Argo LP 624

Introducing Johnny Griffin: Hackensack, N. J., April 17, 1956. Blue Note BLP 1533

A Blowin' Session: Hackensack, N. J., April 6, 1957. Blue Note BLP 1559

The Congregation: Hackensack, N. J., October 23, 1957. Blue Note BLP 1580

Johnny Griffin Sextet: New York, February 25, 1958. Riverside RLP 12-264

Way Out!: New York, February 26 and 27, 1958. Riverside RLP 12-274

The Little Giant: New York, August 4 and 5, 1959. Riverside RLP 12-304

The Big Soul Band: New York, May 24, 1960. Riverside RLP 12-331

Battle Stations (Johnny Griffin/Eddie 'Lockjaw' Davis): Englewood Cliffs, N. J., September 2, 1960. Prestige PRLP 7282

Studio Jazz Party: New York, September 27, 1960. Riverside RLP 12-338

Tough Tenors (Johnny Griffin/Eddie 'Lockjaw' Davis): New York,

November 4 and 10, 1960. Jazzland JLP 31

Griff and Lock (Johnny Griffin/Eddie 'Lockjaw' Davis): New York, November 4 and 10, 1960. Jazzland JLP 42

Live At Minton's (Johnny Griffin/Eddie 'Lockjaw' Davis): New York, January 6, 1961. Prestige PRLP 7191, 7330, 7357

Change Of Pace: New York, February 7, 1961. Riverside RLP 368

Lookin' at Monk (Johnny Griffin/Eddie 'Lockjaw' Davis): New York, February 7, 1961. Jazzland JL 939

Blues Up and Down (Johnny Griffin/Eddie 'Lockjaw' Davis): New York, June 5 and August 17, 1961. Jazzland JLP 60

White Gardenia: New York, July 13, 1961. Riverside RLP 387

The Kerry Dancers – New York, December 21, 1961, January 5, 1962, January 29, 1962. Riverside RLP 420

Tough Tenor Favorites (Johnny Griffin/Eddie 'Lockjaw' Davis): New York, February 5, 1962. Jazzland JLP 76

Pisces (Johnny Griffin/Eddie 'Lockjaw' Davis): New York, May 3, 1962. Riverside OJCCD 1104-2

Full House (Johnny Griffin/Wes Montgomery): Berkeley, Ca., June 25, 1962. Riverside RLP 434

Do Nothin' till You Hear from Me: Berkeley, Ca., June 26, 1962. Riverside RLP 462

Grab This!: Los Angeles, June 28, 1962. Riverside RLP 437

The Swingers Get the Blues too: New York, May 14 and 16, 1963. Atlantic SD 1431

Johnny Griffin Quartet – Jazz Jamboree '63: Warsaw. October 26, 1963. Muza (P) XL 0192, (P) XL 0193

Johnny Griffin Live In London: London, December 11, 15, 29, 1963. Harkit Records HRKCD 8061

Night Lady: Cologne, February 13, 1964. Philips (G) 840447

Johnny Griffin/Art Taylor: April 10, November 28 and December 12, 1964. Storyville STCD 8300

Griff 'n' Bags: Cologne. February 19, 1967; August 13 and 27, 1968; February 2, 1969. Rearward RW 103 CD

The Man I Love: Copenhagen, March 30 and 31, 1967. Polydor 583734, Black Lion BLCD 760107.

A Night in Tunisia: Copenhagen, March 30 and 31, 1967. Freedom FLP 42174

You Leave Me Breathless: Copenhagen, March 30 and 31, 1967. Freedom BLP 30134

Johnny Griffin Meets Dexter Gordon: Rome, January 25, 1968. Lotus LOP 14.082

Lady Heavy Bottom's Waltz: Cologne, August 17, 1968. Vogue (G) LDVS 17164

Blues for Harvey: Copenhagen, July 4, 1973. SteepleChase SCS 1004

Live at Music Inn: Rome, April 7, 1974. Horo HLL 101-10, 101-17

Live in Tokyo: Tokyo, April 23, 1976. Philips RJ 7160

Return of the Griffin: Berkeley, Ca., October 17, 1978. Galaxy GXY 5117

Bush Dance: Berkeley, Ca., October 18 and 19, 1978. Galaxy GXY 5126

Tough Tenors Again 'n' Again (Johnny Griffin/Eddie 'Lockjaw' Davis): Cologne, April 24, 1979. MPS 15283

NYC Underground: New York, July 6 and 7, 1979. Galaxy GXY 5132

To the Ladies: Berkeley, Ca., November 27 and 28, 1979. Galaxy GXY 5139

Summerwind (Johnny Griffin/Monty Alexander/Ray Brown/Martin Drew): Ludwigsburg, April 1980. Jeton 1003312. (Also issued as *Meeting* and with different selections of tracks.)

Call It Whachawana: Berkeley, Ca., June 25 and 26, 1983. Galaxy GXY 5146

Tough Tenors Back Again! (Johnny Griffin/Eddie 'Lockjaw' Davis): Copenhagen, July 10, 1984. Storyville STCD 8298

Three Generations of Tenor Saxophone (Johnny Griffin/Sal Nistico/ Roman Schwaller): Munich, January 11, 1985. JHM Records

Have You Met . . . Barcelona? (Johnny Griffin/Ben Sidran): Barcelona, October 29 and 30, 1987. Orange Blue OB 002 CD

Clémentine – Continent Blue (Johnny Griffin/Clémentine): Barcelona, October 29 and 30, 1987; Paris, December 13 and 14, 1987. Orange Blue OB 004 CD

Take My Hand: Davie, Florida, May 4 and 5, 1988. Who's Who In Jazz, EUCD 1286

Catharsis: Copenhagen, July 15, 1989. Storyville STCD 8306

The Cat: New York, October 26, 28 and 29, 1990. Antilles 848 421-2

Dance of Passion: New York, April 29 and 30, 1992. Antilles 512 604-2

Chicago – New York – Paris: New York, December 4 and 5, 1994. Verve 527 367-2

Johnny Griffin and the Great Danes – Molde, July 17, 1996. Stunt Records STUCD 02012

In and Out (Johnny Griffin/Martial Solal): Paris, June 30 and July 1, 1999. Dreyfus Jazz FDM 36610-2

Close Your Eyes (Johnny Griffin/Horace Parlan): Hamburg, February 2000. Minor Music 801085

Johnny Griffin and Steve Grossman Quintet: Paris, May 28 – 30, 2000. Dreyfus

Compilation

Johnny Griffin – Masters of Jazz Vol. 7: Copenhagen 1964; July 10, 1984; July 15, 1989. Storyville 101 8507

Johnny Griffin DVDs

Jazz Life Vol. 1 – Johnny Griffin Quartet/Richie Cole group: Live at the Village Vanguard, New York, 1981. Storyville 16075

Johnny Griffin Quartet/Mike Mainieri Quintet: Modern Jazz at the Village Vanguard, New York, 1981. Idem Home Video DVD 1139 (Same Johnny Griffin material as on *Jazz Life Vol. 1*)

Jazz Legends – Art Blakey and the Jazz Messengers: Live at the Village Vanguard, New York, 1982. Quantum Leap DJ 869

Compositions by Johnny Griffin

Adrift with You
Alone Again
Always Forever
Ball Bearing
Bee Ees
Black Is the Color of My ....
Blues for Harvey
Blues for Dracula
Blues for Gonzi
Bush Dance
Callitwhachawana
Camp Meeting
Catharsis
Cherry Float
Chicago Calling
Come with Me
Congregation
Continent Blue
Count
Dance of Passion
Dawn
Ding Dong
Do It
Don't Say Goodbye
Fifty Six

For the Love of ...
From Here to There
Grab This!
Green Grow the Rushes
Hey Now
Hipschid
Honey Bucket
Hot Sake
S'il N'y a Pas l'Été
Impro Jazz
The JAMFs Are Coming
Kerry Dancers
Krafty
Lady Heavy Bottom's Waltz
Last of the Fat Pants
Leave Me Alone Blues
Let Me Touch It, Baby
Lollypop
Main Spring
Make Up Your Mind
Mil Dew
Milk Shake
Miriam
A Monk's Dream
Music Inn Blues

Nice and Easy
Not Yet
Off the Wall
Oh, Now I See
Purple Shades
Rhythming
Right Down Front
Same to You
Satin Wrap
Scrabble
63rd Street Theme
Slow Burn
Slukefter Blues
Smoke Stack
Soft and Furry
Suite 1 Southern Airs
Suite 2 Southern Airs
Suite 3 Southern Airs
Suite 4 Southern Airs
Take My Hand
That Party Upstairs
The Cat
The Spider
The Way It Is
To Love
Twins
Waltz for Ma
Waltz with Sweetie
Waltswing
Way It Is
Weasel Walk
What Do You Do?
When You're in My Arms
When We Were One
White Gardenia

Wistful
Woe Is Me
You've Never Been There

With Eddie "Lockjaw" Davis
Again 'n' Again
Layin' on Mellow
Twins

With Joe Morris
Tia Juana

*With Joe Morris
and Bill McLemore*
Jax Boogie

The Johnny Griffin Almanac of Quotes

These are just some of the compositions, extracts from which Johnny Griffin has incorporated into his solos over the years:

The Umbrella Man

Army Air Corps

The Kerry Dancers

Pennsylvania 6-5,000

Swinging on a Star

Rhythm-a-ning

Mairzy Doats

Turkey in the Straw

Rhapsody in Blue

Chimes of Big Ben

Yellow Rose of Texas

Chopin's Polonaise

Cool Blues

Foggy Foggy Dew

The Surrey with the Fringe on Top

Happy Birthday to You

Jumping with Symphony Sid

Manteca

Dark Eyes

Buttons and Bows

Ba Ba Black Sheep

Darling, Je Vous Aime Beaucoup

Did You Ever See a Dream Walking?

Phil the Fluter's Ball

Seven Come Eleven

Nobody Knows the Trouble I've Seen

Pop Goes the Weasel

Yankee Doodle Came to Town

The Campbells Are Coming

Country Gardens

The Song Is You

Mexican Hat Dance

Hut-Sut Rawlson

The Bridal Chorus from Lohengrin (Here Comes the Bride)

Three Coins in the Fountain

Fascinating Rhythm

The Donkey Serenade

Index

Jazz Books from Northway

Ronnie Scott with Mike Hennessey
Some of My Best Friends Are Blues

Derek Ansell *Workout – The Music of Hank Mobley*

Ian Carr *Music Outside*

John Chilton *Hot Jazz, Warm Feet*

Vic Ash *I Blew It My Way: Bebop, Big Bands and Sinatra*

Alan Plater *Doggin' Around*

Peter Vacher *Soloists and Sidemen: American Jazz Stories*

Alan Robertson *Joe Harriott — Fire in His Soul*

Digby Fairweather *Notes from a Jazz Life*

Harry Gold *Gold, Doubloons and Pieces of Eight*

Jim Godbolt *A History of Jazz in Britain 1919–50*

Jim Godbolt *All This and Many a Dog*

Ron Brown with Digby Fairweather
Nat Gonella — A Life in Jazz

Coleridge Goode and Roger Cotterrell
Bass Lines: A Life in Jazz

Forthcoming Jazz Books from Northway

Chris Searle
*Forward Groove: Jazz and the Real World
from Louis Armstrong to Gilad Atzmon*

Graham Collier
The Jazz Composer – Moving Music off the Paper

Peter King
an autobiography

Ron Rubin
A Fanfare of Musical Limericks

www.northwaybooks.com